My Mother is a Chicken

THIS LAND
PRESS

Tulsa, OK

WWW.THISLANDPRESS.COM

Book design and illustrations by Jeremy Luther.

This book was typeset using high-quality, open-source fonts available
from The League of Moveable Type. Support independent design!
Visit Leagueofmovabletype.com.

Body: Linden Hill Regular
Titles: Junction Regular

First Edition, 2012

Printed in the United States of America

ISBN-10:0985848723
ISBN-13:978-0-9858487-2-9

My Mother is a Chicken

is a

Chicken

ESSAYS ON EATING AND DRINKING
FROM THE FIRST DECADE OF ARGENTFORK

BY MARK BROWN

"Does not the noble Marquis of Argentfork give an ox to be roasted whole on the village green when his son, the noble Viscount Silvercoral, comes of age? Beef makes boys into men."

Peter Lund Simmonds, *The Curiosities of Food*

To Kelly—for the endless feast

CONTENTS OF TABLE

Foreword...1

The Peanut Farmer..7
The Days of Wine and Hoses..19
The Coney and the Cantor..33
My Mother Is a Chicken..45
Corn..59
A Quest for Cassoulet...71
The Milking of Chocolate...83
Vintage Smith...97
This Side of Parasite..115
Of Spice and Men..131
An Ode to the Clove..145
The Fat of the Land...157
Oysters...173
Barbecue to the Rescue...183
In the Company of Gin..195
Eggs..207
Waking Blake..221

Selected Reading...237
Acknowledgments...239

FOREWORD

by

Michael Wallis

At last this book is being published. It is long overdue. Finding a publisher willing to bring Mark Brown's words to print was never a problem. Until now, Mark was not ready. Timing, as is the case with all master chefs, is everything to Mr. Brown. Thank all the literary gods above and beyond, now Mark is ready and we are so much the better for it. The wait for this book — *My Mother Is a Chicken: Essays on Eating and Drinking* — sharpened my appetite but it was well worth it. The prose is as satisfying as my mother's Sunday dinners. Now I hunger for more.

I am not even remotely an expert on food but then one does not necessarily have to know much about food to enjoy reading about it. I have made a living as a writer all of my adult life and believe I recognize good writing when I see it. The writing in this book is exceptional. Also, after almost seven decades of consuming everything ranging from all levels of road food, Marine Corps chow, blue plate specials, campfire grub, comfort food, and wild game to haute cuisine, national and regional dishes, and a myriad of concoctions from around the globe, I will tell you straight out that I have never found anyone who does a better job of writing about food and drink and its origins, than Mark Brown.

This should come as no surprise to anyone who knows Mark, someone who obviously is aware that food lends itself to good writing. As the preeminent American food writer M.F.K. Fisher so famously put it long ago, writing about food requires writing about "other, deeper needs for love and happiness ... There is a communion of more than our bodies when bread is broken and wine drunk." In a lifetime spent making her way across the culinary landscape from Provence to the Sonoma Valley, Ms. Fisher redefined food writing with her evocative prose. "A writing cook and a cooking writer must be bold at the desk as well as the stove." Those words could serve as Mark Brown's credo. Indeed, for if there were awards handed out for courageous writing, Mark would have rows of medals pinned to his chest.

Courage — perhaps the most important of the virtues on any level — requires bravery but also honesty, authenticity, and the ability to feel alive and display a true zest for living. And that is just what Mark does in these essays. In so doing, this skilled author helps us understand why he prefers not to be branded as either an epicure of refined taste known as a "gourmet," or, as a "foodie," a childlike label for a particular class of food and drink aficionado. Mark has no need for monikers in telling his stories. He lets his carefully chosen words do all the work. Yet in so doing and with no hint of ego or self-importance, this author truly does open a vein and allows us into his world, a place almost everyone can identify with and savor.

Starting with the first essay, a portrait of his grandfather entitled "The Peanut Farmer," Mark pulls back the canvas tent and gives a peek: "Barney Poole, smelling of perch and hair tonic, fell dead on the dam with a minnow bucket in one hand and a rod in the other. He left a wife, his third, and five children, among them my mother ... It was on Barney's farm that I developed a taste for raw peanuts. In his barn specifically. I spent a lazy afternoon there once, staring up into the rafters, reclining on a burlap bag stuffed with raw peanuts. A bean bag, I reckon. I ate in silence for a good while, studying the studded frame and the light that sifted through the rafters, smelling the cool, dark barn smells. To this day, I cannot eat raw peanuts without smelling dirt. Lost in space, I ate a pound of peanuts. My gut inevitably swelled and I went beyond sick. But I still dig raw peanuts."

This story of a man Mark has called "a great eater of the Canadian River Bottoms," like the other eighteen essays in this book first appeared in *Argentfork*, a quarterly publication Mark has faithfully published for a host of grateful and ardent readers since 2004, while he worked as a designer, editor and food writer for the Tulsa World, and now as the managing editor of This Land, a media company based in Tulsa.

Mark describes *Argentfork* as "a written reflection of a life spent eating and drinking, cooking and thinking. It is an examination of the table beyond methods and ingredients. It gives new meaning to old topics. It goes deeper than most ... It connects the dots between the food we take for granted and its place in the landscape, lineage and lexicon. It is for readers and eaters who enjoy taking their time."

When you devour this collection, you will soon see that Mark has lived up to his promise. Time and again, he delivers — from his "fried chicken exposé" that gives this book its name; to a poignant ode to the "invasive, inescapable, indispensable garlic"; to his San Francisco "martini safari" entitled "In the Company of Gin" to other equally delicious stories of olives, chocolate, pears, and eggs.

So, dear readers pour a beverage of your choice, pull up a comfortable chair, and enjoy this platter of tasty essays Mark Brown has prepared. I promise it will be time well spent and leave you, like me, wanting more.

Bon appétit!

— Michael Wallis, author of *Route 66: The Mother Road*

A nut is the embryo of its plant, the source of its fat and protein. In a drupe, the seed, or kernel, sits within the shell, which resides in the hull, or husk. The edible seeds of almonds, walnuts, pecans, others are encased in the stones of drupes. Plums and peaches are drupes whose fruits we eat and stones we chunk. It is vice versa with certain nuts. The flesh of the walnut we throw to the ground. The kernel of the stone we eat and call a nut. A peanut is more pea than nut—a legume that's found a home in a holiday mix. Peanuts fruit underground. At harvest, they are uprooted and left to dry atop their windrows, the nuts to be harvested, the roots to feed the animals or the earth. Tuskegee University's glossary of 300 products produced from peanuts by George Washington Carver reads like a pantry of antiquity. In Barry Gifford's *Wild at Heart*, manslaughterer Sailor Ripley calls long, leggy Lula Pace Fortune his "Peanut," even as he denudes her, peels back her skin, and sows her seed.

CHAPTER I

THE PEANUT FARMER

Between the chicken coop and the garden stood the house. It was a cobbled-together homestead, part frame, part flagstone, conceived not at once but in a series of afterthoughts. It was cooled by screen doors in summer and, come winter, warmed by a big, bitchin', stone fireplace. From the road, it appeared white, but it fought hard to keep up appearances.

Between the house and a fish pond rose the dam. Dug of earth situated five-some miles southwest of Scipio in Pittsburg County, just north of U.S. 270 in the valley of the silted, stilted Canadian River. It's all there, still—the dam, the chimney, the house, the rocky road that leads to it, the natural gas leases that sprout up around it.

One day when he thought they'd be biting, sometime in his 79th summer, Barney Poole, smelling of perch and hair tonic, fell dead on the dam with a minnow bucket in one hand and a rod in the other. He left a wife, his third, and five children, among them my mother.

Barnett Asbury Poole farmed peanuts and hunted and fished

and ate like a god of his own labor's fruits. He also farmed a bit of sorghum. Sorghum is a cereal that naturally withstands the kind of heat Oklahoma can wreak. Farmers feed it to their cows, of which Barney had a few. Some, not all, varieties of sorghum produce enough juice to allow a sweet, tacky syrup to result. Sorghum, which we ladled on fresh biscuits shiny with wet butter, was for me an acquired taste. After the store-bought flavor of fake maple, sorghum tasted deep, dark, and fermented. It was a flavor profile that I'd not yet cultivated. When it later surfaced in my earliest pints and drams, I wasn't sure enough of myself to admit among drinking buddies that I was reminded, in that malted ale, a little bit of sorghum.

Anyway, I much preferred apple butter on my biscuits. The cinnamon-and-sugar fortified spread that my Mamaw Mary made of her man's modest crop. I ate it all over the dense biscuits and buttery toast of those country breakfasts. Apples were among the few fruits that Barney nurtured on a farm rich with other produce. Plums, pears, peaches—the Elberta variety of his native, southern Arkansas—little else. And even those he let go in time. My mother remembers being sent to the apple tree for some fruit, only to be deterred by a long snake that crept along a long limb within eyeshot. Back on the farm, the stomping ground of her youth, my mother was an Eve to me, slathering the warm bread with that sweet apple butter. It was only after a trip to the persimmon tree that she betrayed my trust.

The problem with a persimmon is its do-or-die nature. Ripe, it's a velvety sweet piece of nearly erotic pulp, orange-yellow and jammy: a ready preserve clinging to a limb. But that pulp is largely fiction, because, for the most part, persimmons are eaten unripe. They must be: it's all that explains the look on nearly everybody's face who has eaten a persimmon. To a person, they curl the tips of their tongues, narrow their eyes, and swear off the bitter pill forever.

The window of opportunity on a ripe persimmon closes as fast as a screen door in a hail storm. I feel strangely blessed to have eaten a ripe persimmon. I got in; I saw the light, enough to say that the persimmon is the oyster of Oklahoma—a copiously strange entity that somebody ate and then re-ate to finally appreciate.

I keep going back, trusting that every next persimmon will rival those beauties I ate stretched across the roof of Barney's white pickup. That persimmon autumn, he'd driven the old Chevy up under the limbs to get us our pick of the fruit. So far, my luck in the supermarket produce aisles has fallen short of that standard.

It was on Barney's farm that I developed a taste for raw peanuts. In his barn, specifically. I spent a lazy afternoon there once, staring up into the rafters, reclining on a burlap bag stuffed with raw peanuts. A bean bag, I reckon. I ate in silence for a good while, studying the studded frame and the light that sifted through its rafters, smelling the cool, dark barn smells. To this day I cannot eat raw peanuts without smelling dirt. Lost in space, I ate a pound of peanuts. My gut inevitably swelled and I went beyond sick. But I still dig raw peanuts. They have a rooty flavor and a carrotty crunch more befitting their status, which is, again, more pea than nut.

Barney had a very great fireplace, wide and tall enough for me to nearly stand up in as a twiggy half-pint. It had no hearth, and the indoor-outdoor carpeting in front of it bore the black craters of errant embers. Sometimes, Barney would roast peanuts in the fireplace and they assumed a new profile—crispy, toasty, fortifying. Archaically, nutmeat: it fits. Of course, he creamed such nuts for butter, and I recall it blonder, oilier, and far less sweet than the processed Peter Pan of my own pantry. Ignorant, I eschewed it.

My father, not a little intimidated by the old man, recalls him roasting sweet potatoes in the ash bed of the fireplace. He'd take the tubers, wrap them tightly in foil, and bury them in the embers to bake. (He also employed a cast-iron kettle for this task.) I was too young to appreciate anything as elemental as a sweet potato roasted in coals and soaked with a large dab of homemade butter, and so it is a flavor I must jealously imagine.

A farm begets butters: apple, peanut, milk. They all smeared that breakfast table. Barney and Mary would take turns churning the milk for butter. The churn was a white clay cylinder with a paddle sticking out the top of it. It resembled a retro toilet-bowl cleaning kit that I've seen at Bed Bath & Beyond. I was mystified to learn that butter would naturally result from a churn of milk pumped patiently enough. I discovered recently that I was righter than I knew, that in fact butter does not necessarily become from a churn.

"You churn it to a point and then you have to stop," a friend affirmed as we breakfasted on granola with skim milk and a cream scone. "Otherwise, you end up with something … else. Something unsuccessful and not butter. My grandparents churned butter."

This friend is a generation ahead of me. His will not be the last to say, as a universal truth, that our grandparents churned their own butter. But mine will be the last. And so I say, with the best memory I can muster, that Barney and Mary's butter never failed, always emerged dense, pale, and richly whipped—like pummeled yolks and sugar, as for a cake batter—and I mistrusted the entire mound of it. In those days, I was a margarine man, pure and simple. I liked my "butter" in refrigerated sticks. Does it matter that I've turned to butter in my maturity? And does it matter that I switched too late to preserve the art of the churn?

One cannot make much money cultivating peanuts for cash crop. Not plowing alone. However, by being a crack shot, a patient fisherman, a keeper of fowl, and an attentive tiller of the native soil, one can eat well. Fish, on the farm, were hard-won and eaten fried. Cornmeal-battered, slightly peppered, salted with vigor—the manner of salting food for which sweet tea was clearly and keenly adopted. The golden-crumbed filets of perch, bass, crappie and catfish piled up on platters lined with paper towels grown greasy from the weight.

We ate swiftly, greedily, while the fish was hot and the hushpuppies crisp. Cornmeal clung to our lips and, in the air, the residues of frying fat, skint fish, and pond water.

Fish is snakes and vice versa. They share the same mystique, swim in the same soup. Fish, for me, will never be gaffing a marlin over the side of a rented boat floating 50 miles out in deepest blue, or dropping a fly on a pebble-bottomed stream against an Ansel Adams backdrop, or a flipping, twisted torso yanked from a jellied lake through a perfect ice circle inches thick. Fish, first and last, is snakes.

Native to my grandfather's land, as native as Choctaws, bobwhites, and the timeless convicted of Big Mac, the state penitentiary, is the yellow-black cottonmouth moccasin. I was around fish and their environs often enough in the formative years to develop a sense for them keener than fear. Once, I saw something dart into the rushes under a bridge, followed it out of curiosity, and ended up kicking it into the creek when it began to coil around my ankle. It had double-backed on me as I leaned out over the reeds for a closer look.

One hot day, I heard a kitten's tender whine and followed it to the shallows of Barney's pond, only to find a cottonmouth agape, exposing the bubble-gum puff of its mouth, head back, fangs postured for defense. And, off of it, the smell. It is the aroma of the earth's underbelly—of funk, mud, and mint. Where I smell that, I smell fish.

Barney was a man of few words. Hence, when he moved, it was with a communicative air. The weight in his step, his tongue as it rolled across the paper of a hand-rolled smoke, the slickness of the fingers that steered an earthworm up a brass hook—these gestures spoke in place of words. His speech had a spare quality to it, and he used words to make a statement, not fill a silence. It was an unintended thrift, I think. He'd simply grown accustomed, over the years, to letting other people talk too much.

He spoke loudest when, one day, he took aim on a snake coiled on a large piece of Styrofoam anchored on the far side of the pond for no reason anybody could clearly explain. It was a white chunk of junk, but the snake took to it, its body rolling gently in a mid-morning sun. I was fishing with my mother and father, one of whom tolerated snakes. She, on the other hand, reeled from them as she might the devil himself. It was she who sent me to the house for the master.

"Mark, go get Daddy and tell him there's a snake."

I told him and he climbed from his chair the way glaciers climb hills. "I'll be there directly."

That was a favorite word of his. It meant whenever, but for sure. Finally, that snake would die by one shot from the rifle of a near-blind man who spoke not a single word as he approached the bank and prepared to take aim, except one: "Where?"

The farm afforded taboos in spades. There were dark places— forbidden outposts, aged lean-tos, and grub-thick compost— where I never ventured for fear of body and soul. The chicken coop, the vacant stable, the vast pasturage that stretched back and beyond the house, into the woods of Sasquatch, many snakes, and the dank banks of Muddy Boggy Creek. Similarly, I never entered the smokehouse, no more than just a peek in the door when Barney might open it to retrieve a piece of pork. Next to the smokehouse was the well, and so I did my damage there, tossing down chunks of chat from the rugged driveway simply to hear the splashes clang in the dark core of the earth. By compromise, I kept well clear of the hickory-polluted house of pig. But I did eat of its contents.

The bacon on Barney's table bore the rind trimmed from store bacon. I loved to chew the fat off the rind until it softened enough to be either swallowed or strung across the plate in gristled ropes. I learned, at that table, to regard bacon, eggs, and biscuits as manna, with the syrup or sorghum on the biscuits the dipping sauce for the bacon. Asian cuisine has taught me this pursuit of salty sweet is nothing less than Zen.

Barney spooned redeye gravy over his ham. The eye in redeye gravy refers to the swirling, dark cloud of rich coffee as it emulsifies with the pan grease into a salty glaze. If you find redeye gravy outside of the South, it's because somebody took it there.

My own taste for coffee was cultivated in those days, seated attentively next to Mary in the early hours that only children and old folks rise and shine. She poured it into plastic green cups, in small quantities doctored heavily with fresh milk and sugar. I waited for it to cool and drank it down like soda. "I drink coffee!" I told my mother in a half-confession, half-proclamation the first time she entered the kitchen to find me wired. I was anxiously proud to be drinking coffee at age 5. Today, I omit the sugar and apologize to no one.

Not all the beasts on the farm slithered and swam. I got near enough to a hog once to be scared stiff. I rode with Barney on the back of the tractor, hugging him around the chest, the smell of worn overalls and yesterday's sweat rising off his neck. I held tight as he wheeled the tractor into the pen to feed the beast. It was a Jimmy Dean hog, splotched black-and-white and the biggest, gnarliest thing I'd gotten that close to in my young life. Barney tossed ears of raw corn onto the mud and the hog swallowed them on sight. It moved not without grace, and with the nervous force of a young contender. My mother's mother sewed sacks out of cheesecloth for casing sausage. All the offal went to Ed and Gertie Carson down the road.

It seemed a sad existence, trapped in all that mud and shit and spent corn, but I don't know. Hogs are said to wallow, which by definition means to roll oneself about in a lazy, relaxed, or ungainly manner. I can read happiness in that.

My dad tells a story of taking the same trip I took, but not to feed. This time, Barney pulled a pallet behind the tractor. He had corn but this time, instead of tossing it onto the ground, he scattered it across the pallet. When the pig approached to graze, Barney blasted him in the back of the head with a pistol. The pig fell to the pallet, hoof-up, and the old man pocketed the gun and turned the tractor toward the slaughterhouse—about as much procession as a pig is likely to get.

A random memory: Two young cowboys tending a barbecued cow in a pasture at night. The lights in the wired yard of Big Mac loomed in the distance. The boys talked about the next day's festivities and the crickets chimed in. They had to have been cooking beef for the prison rodeo is all I can think. We squatted around a fire and the young lads answered my dad's questions politely, quietly, their faces lit up by firelight. They wore hats and chambray shirts. They could have been angels, like the one that appeared when the disciples went to roll back the stone.

The barnyard harbored many animals in its day, but only the pointers—I remember three or four dogs, but only one name, Happy, that I think they shared—made pets. All other hoof and down were destined for victuals. Chickens were always giving up the ghost in a fat-hot frying pan. Cut-up parts of bird, in the traditional eighths, piled in the sink to be rinsed after a good plucking. My mother fries a mean chicken and this is where she learned to do it. Pan-fried, in Crisco shortening, with a floured skin that mostly browned but also went black in places, from the hot spot of the seasoned skillet. Fried chicken on the bone, fried potatoes, fried okra, and sliced tomatoes with salt and pepper, sweet tea. Food with soul, if not soul food.

I wasn't supposed to, but I saw my Papaw cleave a turkey one fall day, watched it do a hopeless, headless dance around the yard before dropping dead under the great oak where the wooden swing twisted like a feather in rough weathers. My mom caught me peeking and closed the window on the rest of the show, but I saw enough to write a story about it many years later, among my first ever for print and still among the proudest.

D ays in the country are destined to be spent on sustenance. You seem always to be thinking, talking, planning, procuring, or worrying about food. Are the berries ripe and sweet for picking? Will the boys kill enough birds for a proper feed? Have we peeled the beans, boiled the turnips? Will there be enough fish to go around? What would Jesus do, I'd wonder, with five channel catfish and two skillets of cornbread? Fresh experience has taught me that Sundays in Pittsburg County vary not much from Sundays in the Languedoc region of France, where I lived for a year. Both consist of large lunches of too many courses followed by, in season, football and, always, naps.

Both of my grandfathers were deacons in the local Baptist affiliate and neither of them drank. I never saw Lloyd or Barney take a single drop. Strange, admirable even, but not a habit I inherited. Barney did, however, chew tobacco. Not from a can or a pouch but from a dark plug he cut with a pocket knife during idle times in front of the fireplace or on the porch. That plug he cut for chew looked to me like a brownie and I longed for a taste.

Barney came to visit us in the city rarely. I remember only one occasion. It was not long after we'd moved into a new house on a hill in south Tulsa called Shadow Mountain. In town, he was even more quiet and aloof than in the country. He took his early mornings out in the backyard, in a lawn chair, to escape the howl of the air-conditioning. It was sirens, not heat, that finally drove him back indoors.

I don't recall sharing meals, though I know we must have. People still ate largely at a table then, and my mom set it with solid, if post-modern, homecooking. It wasn't my grandparents' table: it wasn't spread with the unprocessed stuffs that I found foreign.

She modernized her table with packets of Rice-A-Roni, cartons of glazed frozen doughnuts, boxes of sugared cereals. Probably for my sake, and my young brother's, but my mother's too, who must have had fresh memories of the made-from-scratch life. I can't imagine what Barney thought of such fare.

It is difficult to know what one gleans from one's ancestors, what habits are assumed, what tendencies inherited. I've been told that I have Lloyd's temper. And I did, while it mattered. But a temper needs a high-pressure cell in order to combust, and I've long since given up the competitive sports and scenarios that caused me to rage. Time, not self-control, has diffused the inner storm.

Time's like that. Left alone, it will render most things that want to challenge it, deem it catastrophic and supernatural when in fact it's really just making up for lost time. Time takes the tips off peaks, shallows the seas, tightens the days. Time brings into focus what the conscience cannot. And so it must be time, and the full-circled aspect of it, that sharpens the image of what Barney meant to me. I had to get three decades away from it in order to grasp its significance. Had to cook my own meals, buy my own meat, find my own way to value the country boy that came two generations ahead of me, he with his baited hooks and chicken bleedings and seasonal pickings. Out of Arkansas, of all places.

Barnett is one of those old, old names that nobody invokes anymore. It means "noble man." Versus nobleman. If there's a difference.

L'hiver

In 2002, the year of "freedom fries," we lived in a tiny wine village in the poorest part of France. Saint-Chinian, and the Languedoc generally, was experiencing its coldest winter in years. We settled into the two-story house at 13, rue de l'Amour in time for the Christmas oysters and the frozen pipes. The only heat came from a pair of electric units capable of exhausting a life savings in an afternoon. In lieu of that, we'd roast our dinner and leave the oven door open, then shut ourselves inside the kitchen and play cards and read books and make plans until bored enough to brave the stone-cold stairs for bed. In those cold, early days, we padded our bones with Cote d'Or chocolate and glasses of Le Chant de Marjolaine, our lips purpling probably from the wine but likely from the cold.

At Marseille, we had to be told, there was snow.

CHAPTER II

THE DAYS OF WINE AND HOSES

They are not long, the days of wine and roses:
Out of a misty dream
Our path emerges for a while, then closes
Within a dream.
—Ernest Dowson

Les printemps

It was Thursday, a market day, and the Place Marché buzzed with basket-carrying moms, grandmères and British expats. I was shopping for dinner, but it assembled itself: firm, new potatoes from the father-son team whose vegetables still wore dirt; a clump of onions whiter than a wedding; a hard, pink head of rose du Tarn garlic, from Toulouse-Lautrec country, cloves the size of cicada. For the salad, I found a fistful of young arugula from the organic farmer-chef, his wolf's eyes and Kurt Cobain hair bringing to mind one of Queen Margot's several lovers. Tiny snails would infiltrate the leaves and find a home there. Often, I didn't discover them until they gave between my teeth in a sandy crunch.

I stocked up on olives—Niçoise, picholine, Greque au naturelle, and the famed green goddess, the Lucques de Bize—because it was the Mediterranean and because of how olives look and taste next to the duck: a breast hibernating beneath a skin of fat a quarter-inch or more, far too much coat for such a day.

Spring had blown wide open, ordnance above the sprouting vines, blasting the blues skies with a tingly light. Winter was over, not to return, not for one day, and the pollen in the air gave me a hunger for honey, which we'd taken to drizzling over month-old goat cheese.

I made my way home, past the bike shop and the bakery, to deposit the produce and check the cellar, a head-bumping wedge of a space—carved out by the stone-and-wood staircase—that never warmed up. I added bottles one, two at a time, given the space, our budget, the ticking clock. It is fortified by offerings from the local wineries, of which there are dozens, but other Languedoc labels make a showing: Corbieres, Faugeres, Minervois, Fitou and Limoux, too, all the region has to offer. But a big region it is, and a lifetime—never mind a year—is hardly enough to get to the bottom of that barrel.

Our few dozen bottles slept silently, awaiting the dinner hour. I took a fresh count: For now, it wasn't the cellar that needed replenishing. It was the jug.

Our rented rooms were so near the co-op that, come summer, the clinking of bottles being filled made for a nice wake-up call. The tink-ding of battalions of bottles was a seamless march, like the vinification of a thousand ripe fields.

I pushed open the door of the co-op and was baptized yet again in the yeasty, musty essence of fermented fruit. "Vingt village … une appellation," went the tagline. Twenty villages under one name: vin du Saint-Chinian. It is among the appellation's most ancient producers, with vines as old as the Via Domitia, the Roman road to Spain.

I told the clerk to fill her up with the grand cru, making sure to say please. I can afford premium here; the regular is a less-refined, 10 percent-by-volume plonk a spit above dregs. She took my five-liter jug, inserted the nozzle and pumped the good stuff. Wine frothed to the lip and stopped on a dime. I paid my eight euros, hefted the jug, and felt welling in the depths of me a dark, delicious secret, one that we shared many nights mostly alone.

But they were not long, those days of wine and hoses.

I'd just bookmarked myself halfway through John O'Hara's *The Hat on the Bed* and decided to make tea: a fruity cup of Earl Grey that we bought in Narbonne, the ville of Zacarias Moussaoui, the only person charged in the U.S. for the Sept. 11 attacks. Narbonne market—a grand pavilion that begins with flowers and escalates into fresh eels—is home to Chez Jo, Jo being a stiletto-wearing wisp of a thing who'll cook a steak for you if you find one to your liking in the bloody butchers' stalls. She'll pour you a pastis, too, and never mind the hour.

Between sips of tea (and thick dabs of Nutella on baguette), I pondered how to cook that night's duck. If I sauteed it, I could use the fat to moisten the potatoes. On the grill, I'd get the good, charry flavor but pay the price in a near-inferno of hissing fat. If I don't incinerate it on the grate, the deep-red breast resembles not a bird but a rich, tangy steak that cries for and gets a generous dollop of Dijon mustard.

I finished the tea and padded across the tile and terrazzo to the mini cave beneath the stairs. For duck, something local in the glass: maybe the Berloup Terroir or Domaine Rimbert's Travers des Marceaux or Mas Champart's Causse du Bousquet. Or all three. Together, they don't make 15 euros. To whet, I poured a glass of the house red and rinsed my mouth of Earl Grey. The flavor of earth and fruit rushed simply and sanely in, around and down. I turned on France Musique just in time (6 p.m. nightly) to catch Zoot Sims playing George Handy's "Let's not waltz tonight," the intro to Alain Gerber's program *Jazz est un romain*. Between numbers, Gerber weaves the story of a jazzcat named Joe and, just like a novel, sunlight flashed off the stones of the petit patio enclave where we dine and I've decided on the duck:

Grilled.

My wife—and partner in this emigration—met a couple, Aimée and Clement, who tended a garden down by the river. She took me there as the cherries were ripening and we stood under Aimée's tree chewing cherries and spitting stones as the blossoms snowed down around us. On our way out of the garden, Clement tore a branch of laurel from a tree and handed it to me. I took the offering and hung it on the wall of our kitchen. It was bay leaf enough for a year. Clement's laurel lent the most sublime tincture to a pan of rabbit paella, or a veal chop marinated overnight and grilled over coals, both the bay and the veal waging battle for the turf of most delicate.

l'Ete

It was rare when I didn't cook in my borrowed pocket of France, given the options, the many mysteries of hoof, fin, and feather, and the vast vineyards for accompaniment. Cooking is a form of proof, and in every bottle a message. But it was Robert Eden's birthday—when the moon is always full—and so I put away my knife.

We were drinking sparkling wine when Eden's moon climbed out of the Mediterranean, over the earth, a red-orange Frisbee in need of a toss. As it rose, it grew bright enough to light up the whole of the Minervois, our wine neighbor to the west. We walked in its glow, an after-party march to the top of Chateau Combebelle, with Eden—nephew of Sir Anthony Eden, Earl of Avon, Prime Minister of England in the wake of Churchill—cutting a swath.

We basked in the brilliance of that moon, on the strength of grilled mackerel, shoulder of lamb, roasted chickpeas, several of Eden's many labels and one not his: a carafe of Chateauneuf-du-Pape that made the rounds sometime before the cheese. Drinking the wine of the Avignon popes—that vintage, anyway—gave this Protestant boy serious cause for conversion.

On our walk, Eden pointed to a place, on a rise several crags over, that he said was the highest in the Minervois, then to a patch of earth that he'd soon be planting.

"With what?" I asked.

"Grenache," he said. "Probably."

My mind, if not mouth, was still tasting Chateaneuf, a Rhone classic cut heavily from the cloth of grenache, and with more suppleness. The popes had a leg up on Eden, but I respected him too much as host and near-nobleman to compare tasting notes. He'd spoken earlier of American "cowboys"—"Like Bush," the Brit said. "And that Bernard Ebbers, he's one"—while the Mars-like moon rose above him, crowning his thinning, blond pate the way Fra Angelica anointed the apostles, in a halo of color and circumference. Eden's moon came full circle just as Benji, the chateau's keeper of the vines, emerged from the kitchen, carting a platter of grilled fish.

"Oh!" he said, staring southward into the sky. "I thought it was a joke, that moon thing!"

It was, and on us.

The moon went down and the sun came out and we went for a picnic on the beach at Sete. A pain baigne and a Roquebrun rosé. To make the sandwich, you lay slices of day-old baguette in a deep dish. Then, you drown them—in tuna and anchovies, capers and olives, thinly sliced tomatoes and thinner onions, plenty of olive oil and a splash of wine vinegar. After lunch, you can wade into the sea and wash your hands in the waist-deep salt of the Mediterranean. At Sete, you can wade a hundred yards out without ever losing bottom, then the first outer bank rises and you can go a few more yards after that and then you must swim.

Back on the beach, we rinsed our greasy lips with the pink wine of Roquebrun and, after some shuteye, started combing the sands for beach glass. They are lovely curiosities: deep-green, sandblasted shards whose edges have been muted by the infinite toss of time and tide. They are generally small pieces, thumb-sized and bottle-thick, remnants of a whole that once held who knows what—cheap Bordeaux, Coteaux du Languedoc, perhaps picpoul de pinet, the local white that drinks so well with the fruits of the sea.

Again, who knows. By the time you have collected it among the rounded stones of Sete, it is yours to say what vintage the glass once colored. I imagine great Burgundies, tossed overboard by Japanese connoisseurs, or young, raw Herault vintages warmed by bonfires, hoisted by crusaders fresh from a Béziers bloodletting. Drunk, they flung the empties into the sea—dregs of ripe, gamy mourvèdre sloshing in the vessel bottoms—and slept where they fell, the sea walls at Sete catching the last shred of sunlight as it dipped below the horizon.

In my village market, cheese was the last stall. (Usually. The last week of August, we bought a watermelon from the North African who lives near the river, one street over from our rue de l'Amour, whose stall only comes out in summer. I pointed to one and he lifted the melon as though pulling a bowling ball off the rack. That's when the bottom fell out of it, the matter splattering at his feet. "C'est pourquoi ils appellent melon d'eau!" he let out, his French coated with cigarettes and sands.)

My cheese man made the twice-a-week trip from up near Roquefort, carting with him several samples of the legendary, veiny, sheep's milk blue. But Roquefort is not the only kid on the block. It's an architecture like no other, this cheese case, the pyramids, squares, wedges, towers and rounds rising in a decadent unity. My man cuts pieces gently to order, tucks them into white paper and asks, "Un autre choix?" His cautious, carving moves, his white smock and his smooth, gray hair, remind me of a dentist I once trusted but no more. With summer visitors en route, I scouted another selection.

For a time in the winter, on the heels of a visit to Laguiole in the volcanic hills of Aveyron, I swore off cheese. It started with a country lunch in a warm café, migrated to a cattle auction replete with steaming dung, and ripened head long in a video at the AOC Laguiole visitor's center, where the smell of raw milk unearthed in me some distant, yakking yaw. But now it was summer, and I chose a nice, snowy Chaource.

The market was never more alive than in June. Fruit fell in droves, and a woman we knew with elephantine legs had boiled a thousand apricots into a thick, orange soup. You could smell the pot several stalls away. I asked for a pint and she ladled the fruit into a plastic container, spilling some of the napalm onto her fat hands. (I confided to her back in the winter that I'd kill to get my own hands on a whole foie gras and she admitted to knowing just the place. She'd take us there, she told me, and share with me her *methode culinaire* for preparing an entire goose liver. It never happened.) She handed me the *abricots* and took my euro. The container sagged from the heat. Home, we smeared the still-warm spread onto peasant bread painted thickly with Normandy butter.

Friends arrived from Seattle and I wasted no time plying them with the local delicacies: crispy duck confit, young chevre, grilled lamb, even a gut-wrenching drive to Spain, down the Costa Brava into Catalonia for fresh fish and crustaceans. Afterward, we bathed, in the same, calm waters that aroused the young Dalí.

Then we picnicked at Roquebrun, on the dry cobblestones of the summer-clear River Orb, with the famed ruin towering like a flagpole in some rustic centerfield. I composed a Caprese salad of overlapping slices of tomato and goat cheese tucked with whole basil leaves and dressed in balsamic—the remnants of a bottle we balanced on the train from Florence—and the green-apple tasting olive oil of the nearby cooperative, L'Oulibo. To stave off the heat, we drank rosé from a vineyard likely within view. Cynthia, with the form of a 20-game winner, hurled stones into the river. Bret slathered so much Dijon onto a slice of bread that it brought tears.

Stolen time flies faster than any other and too soon we were in the car to Lyon, for a two-star lunch at Leon de Lyon and then to deposit our pals on a Paris-bound train. Summer was still a week away but in many ways it was finished. Kelly and I drove back home, down the Rhone Valley with the windows rolled down, the hottest day of the year making convection of the Jetta.

A week later, I'd wear fleece to the Bastille Day celebration in the local rugby stadium, the temperature dipping into the 50s, which I still counted in Fahrenheit. Cold and lonely—Kelly was in Paris with a friend, dancing on a playfully crowded bridge between arrondissements, monitoring patriotic explosions that lit up the Eiffel—I slunk home to warm up with a solo dram of Armagnac.

The glass, now six months in the cupboard, had gone half empty.

What came between summer and fall was the vendage, the picking. My missus picked days on end, taking pictures between handfuls, though I picked but once: a tepid September morning, among a group of more polished Polish, Dutch, and Montreal grapemen and women. By lunch, my back was bent like Hugo's hunchback and my hands were pockmarked, by countless snips from a set of pruning shears, unable as I was to decipher my fingers from vine stems. All that saved me was a field of cinsault grapes, clusters I tried to clip by falling desperately again to my weakened knees only to have sprightly Monsieur Quartironi, in this his 40th vintage, put me out of my misery. "These grapes," he said softly, "we eat." So we did, the lot of us, the entire field silent but for the sound of grape pips being spit, p-tuh, p-tuh ... p-tuh, p-tuh. Silent, except for the slurping of sweet cinsault grapes the size of walnuts, a thing so sweet it sugar-coated my dreams from that September forward, to all the Septembers to come.

l'Automne

I met an old woman on the bridge, staring glumly into the ankle-deep Vernazobre, and stopped to ogle beside her. "*Pas peche la*," she said. Indeed, the trout were not running. I passed the church and the intimidating butcher's where I used to shop and turned left on the rue d'Eglise. Overhead, somebody's laundry swung in the current of air that cascaded through the narrow streets of stone anchoring ancient spires. I made a right and was at the threshold of Monsieur et Madame Peyras. With seven butchers in a town of 1700 souls, it took me awhile to find Chez Peyras— their shop hiding all the way on the other side of town, a good four minutes' walk from my doorstep—and I was wasting no time sampling their coffers.

Their chalkboard was a daily refreshing of regional farm fare: bacons and hams, filets of pork, breasts and shanks of veal, and beef in oddball cuts. Dried sausage dangled from the ceiling in molded ropes. Behind the glass, chickens drooped from a recent wringing, their delicate combs parted to one side and a few stubborn quills clinging at the leg and wing tips. Eggs, maybe theirs, were piled in a straw basket atop the case, fresh enough to need no refrigerant.

I spotted a thoroughbred of a rabbit, flayed out with the innards exposed as proof of freshness. I was about to ask for it in pieces for a sauté or perhaps a paella, and monsieur would flip the switch on the table saw to cross-cut a carcass into a dozen meaty chunks. But before I could pull the trigger, madame emerged from the cold storage with a whole lamb slung over her shoulder. I'd ordered five of her chops instead.

"*Pour deux personne?*" monsieur asked, whacking away at the opposite counter on a side of beef. Yes, I said, just we two.

A couple of weeks back, I ordered a chunk of pork to roast and he raised an eyebrow at me. Sure enough, the next day, we ate leftovers. Ever since, I tell him only what I want and how many will be at table and let him determine the size of the cut. Like Pascal, his math does not fail.

But these chops are small and five is assurance. And there is no explaining the more dire predicament that I am a traveler, a taster hell-bent on consumption, with a limited time to sample all that the Languedoc has to offer. I am an anomaly, and five chops when four would suffice are the luxury I afford myself.

Smiling at my assuredness, Madame sliced in learned motions and held out to me the red, royal chops for inspection, delicately and tenderly and with, no kidding, a wink.

Our autumn has come, and clouds have dimmed any view of Le Caroux, a woman of a mountain that reclines several kilometers north, her nose and breast and toes providing relief against the deep blue of the Midi, a blue gone stone gray. But the vine leaves are red, orange, and yellow—a colorful, knee-high New Hampshire.

We were taking in the fall festival in Berlou, drinking leathery, plummy syrah, when it came, the deja vu—a burnt aroma of coal-roasted chestnuts, not unlike a death's bed, with a dense nut pulled from a rich, acrid smoke. Roasted chestnuts are more romantic than delectable, but these meats were sweeter than those we ate in Toulouse on New Year's Eve 2001, roasted with great aplomb by a band of Catalans worthy of a Rick Steeves video. The Place du Capitole, hazy with the smoke of cauldrons, was to become the scene of the crime: a bottle rocket glancing off my boot; a kicked, empty magnum of cheap bubbly chiming across the paving stones; a magenta smoke-bomb plume; and a black sedan being bashed to bits by a fist-waving gang—a spidered windshield violently ushering in another year.

January came rushing back, and this is how a life, a stolen year from beginning to end, would come to be bookmarked—by the caramelized crunch of a toasted chestnut.

I drank a last café noir at the Café Vernazobre and Kelly took pictures. I wore a cotton turtleneck that sagged from its own, unwashed weight. It was official: French coffee is unremarkable. Three men drank—two cafés blanc and one liqueur—and the light of the last day began to dawn.

It was a Thursday, a day that, to a tourist on sabbatical, lost its luster as the day between humpday and weekend. We walked through the market, no basket in hand, bags packed and waiting at what was still home for another hour. Otherwise, business as usual. The tourists were long gone, as were the melons, tomatoes and mushrooms. "That's the last of the Citou onions," I recalled John, my man in Minervois, saying the winter before, and that's how they go: sautéed until just black at the edges, then strewn across an otherwise insidious pizza from the cart down by the rivier. Sweet, tender, fresh, singular.

And gone.

My best friend in adolescence came into my life from Farmington, New Mexico, the closest city of any kind to the American Four Corners. One of the first things we debated, in that youthful, oblivious sort of way, was chili. "Chilies are green," he argued, describing in plural what I only knew in bowlfuls. "Then they dry and they turn dark red." We were getting somewhere, but I didn't realize how close we'd gotten. The chili I knew—slathered on hot dogs, oozing from enchiladas, dabbed with sleeves of saltines—was a stew, impure and simple. That it came from a pepper was news to me. To see chilies in chili, you have to see in shades, in halftones. To imagine the peppers turned to powder turned to stew, you have to believe in magic. "Red?" I said, more curious than ever. "You mean brown."

CHAPTER III

THE CONEY AND THE CANTOR

Paint peels from the old hotel that floats above the Coney Island Hot Weiner Shop like a bobber over a baited hook. A hand-lettered sign at the door reads, "No change without purchase." Riders and hangers-on from the bus depot across the street saunter in and out, reeling and dealing.

I sit with my back to the wall, hammering away on three "regulars." The chairs are the classic, wooden, school kind, the ones with the writing slab on the right, leaving the left arm to idle or do the devil's work. Who operates with one hand like that besides children and chain gangs? A roomful of frank-fisted carnivores leans over greasy, foam trays dotted with chili drippings, as they might have over Big Chief tablets.

Three coneys are about right. Four takes me to the edge. I could imagine eating 10. I can eat a coney in four bites, gluttonously, five otherwise. At the Coney Island, three or more earn you a free drink, any size.

A wild-eyed couple approaches the register, pulling dollars and cents from frayed pockets as the cashier patiently waits. They sport a long-past-wanted look, like refugees of the Manson Family Compound. They pay, find adjacent seats, and tear into lunch elbows out.

Under the window, on the steel grill, wieners, once perfect and pink, are turned until they barely warp. Wieners come packaged pre-cooked; the fire is for steaming, coloring and caramelizing. They sizzle and pulse on the griddle until their number is called and off they come, like ducks in a midway moat. Every so often, quite often, a box is torn open and a new stack of hot-pink meat rolls onto the rack.

Since the early 1900s, at least, a coney is a hot dog that hails from Coney Island. At Coney Island Hot Weiner Shop, since 1926. "We haven't changed a bite," goes the old tagline, but they did add grated cheese, somewhere around the time of Donna Summer. As a meal, there isn't much to say: coneys, chips, Pepsi. It's a sparse menu with a few glaring intrusions: spring water for 90 cents, cappuccino for a buck. Jars of cayenne pepper for $2.25, which they'll refill for 50 cents.

A coney is also a burrowing, rabbit-like mammal that's called a hyrax in the Mediterranean and southwest Asia and a pika in the Rocky Mountains. A coney is also a colorful reef fish of the Caribbean.

A "regular" is a wiener swabbed in yellow mustard (yellowed by turmeric powder) and buried in steaming chili and minced onions. Cheesefood has been the condiment of choice since the '70s, and all but the old-timers gobble it up. Three regulars and a drink cost me $4.03. The 97 cents rattles into a metal cup attached to the register, leaving the diner to mine the change, for old time's sake.

The bite meets all the savory requirements: soft, salty, warm, and snappy. I don't concern myself with a wiener's contents, knowing that most of it comes from a pig, a godly creature, preserved with a few chemicals. I live with the chemicals as I will die with them—in moderate intake until one day the math catches up.

i. *The Science of 14-1*

Jim Economou reminds me of somebody. A more-relaxed, less-paranoid Christopher Lloyd, maybe. His skin is a soft white, his hair whiter. His eyes glow like diamonds, or finely diced onions. He's a life-long Tulsan who lacks the accent, his voice, like his face, not easily placed. In old photos, he is svelte, the shoulders—now slightly slumped—arcing in Grecian proportion.

Jim's made a lifetime in a hot dog stand. More than, it seems. He'd have long retired by now, but the sons who would have stepped in took up ophthalmology and law instead. Their sons were to have been the first to break ranks. "It wasn't supposed to happen this quickly," Jim says of his heirs. "They leaped ahead a generation."

And so, the language of chili and cheese ends here, in the desk-chair next to me, with James Economou. Not sure where to begin, I start with size. Wieners that become coneys are made of minced beef or pork or both and are designated by how many of them it takes to make a pound: 8-1, 12-1, 20-1 and so on. Jim Economou buys a 16-1.

"It used to be a little bigger," he says. "Not in circumference, but a little longer. Like a 14-1."

The wiener his dad insisted on was even bigger and, Jim contends, better. "Back then, we had a really good wiener that was made by a guy over on Boulder, at the viaduct. When I say good, now, this guy was a superb sausage maker. In the old days, you had people who had just come from Germany working in those plants. In think it was Swift."

The difference in circumference and such can be subtle. Much of the weight is lost on the grill, where the fat sizzles and rides off on tiny molecules that charge the air and film the fixtures. The weight that separates a 14 from a 16 is lost in space.

"Dad instructed them to make an 80-20 beef-to-pork ratio. The pork, he felt, gave it that extra taste. A smoother taste. The beef was always a little on the tough side. You have to be very careful when you're cooking an all-beef wiener."

Christ the Elder, the first Tulsa Economou, had the sort of face—Charlie Chaplin moustache, immovable jaw, paper cap set militarily back—that would send a young diner behind his father's pant leg for cover. Not to mention a vendor.

"That 80-20 wiener had no cereal, no junk, no nothing. Beef and pork. He told them that under no circumstances would he accept any chicken or turkey in the product. 'I'll get something else,' he'd tell them."

Jim points to the window, to where "Coney Island Hot Weiners" is painted in red and white. Hardly anybody mentions the misspelling anymore. "Always," he says, "in a diphthong like that, you pronounce the second vowel. But he did this in order to get a copyright on the name."

Christ shipped to New York in the wake of World War I. Before joining the clan that would create the Tulsa coney shop, he drove spikes and, for a while, worked in a Sheboygan slaughterhouse. You say Christ with a short i, like mist.

Intermezzo

That old Swift plant Jim spoke of stood under the bridge at 2 S. Boulder Ave. Near there, in early 2007, a man and wife headed to the Day Center for the Homeless were climbing over a rail car to get across the tracks when the car lurched. The wife fell to the ground and tumbled beneath the car. The wheels turned and took her head off. The train, headed from Memphis to Los Angeles, had stopped to switch crews.

ii. Conduct Becoming

It's too early for coneys so Jim and I have the room to ourselves. Empty, it is a classroom: polished, chlorinated, bright and ready for young butts. He's talking about Hindemith, the composer, when a woman on the phone orders several dozen franks. "She's buying 65," a guy in a paper cap says. "No drinks."

Jim's mind moves behind his eyes. "Sixty-five times a dollar and a quarter," he says after a few seconds. "Where were we? Oh yeah."

He says if you don't understand why a conductor matters then you never saw one like Paul Hindemith, the great German. Someone who knew the music he was conducting inside and out. "Oh, my goodness, that Hindemith," Jim says with a marvelous shake of the head.

"Whatever they were playing, he knew the piece, its history, and how it fit in the moment. He'd do it the way the composer would have liked it to be heard. You have to relay all of this understanding to the orchestra. It isn't just an appreciation of instruments—it's knowing people.

"This may be the only thing left, outside of football teams, where the entire group is wired to one person."

During World War II, Jim played viola in the 7th Army symphony orchestra, based out of Stuttgart. The 7th Army symphony played only one hall filled to less than capacity, the day the Russians invaded Hungary. "Sixteen people showed up. We said, 'Should we play?' They said, 'Yes, play. Play!' I think it may have been Aachen, but all over Germany they came to hear the music. They adored the music. Oh, their reaction. We were beside ourselves."

The 7th Army symphony crossed Europe giving concerts, with the charge of playing as often as possible in Germany. To show another side of the American G.I., Jim explains it. Everywhere but Hungary, they packed the house. "When I say packed! Oh, my, even the aisles had to be emptied after a performance. It was an amazing bunch. All of us had degrees."

Jim bought a Leica on his Army per diem and photographed his European tour. Now, the Leica sits in a case in the top of his closet. "It represents this beautiful period of 18 months traveling Europe, courtesy of the U.S. Army."

Jim came hard by the beauty, learning the forms of music from a father whose intensity made up for his shortcomings. Nearly blind from birth, Christ Economou learned to cant by devouring the canon, practicing the 12 books of the Greek Orthodox cantor until they became second sight. One volume a month, month after devoted month.

"You say this is amazing," Jim says. "It isn't amazing. But I'll tell you why I did not become a cantor. He'd say to me, get a book off the shelf. 'Crack it open and start reading. Anywhere.' I'd start and he'd begin to follow me, canting, or chanting. 'Crack another.' 'No, papa,' I'd beg him. 'Open it,' he'd say. I'd open it and start to read. Same thing. All 12 volumes. But instead of encouraging me, it had the opposite effect. There ain't no way I was going to follow that.

"The thing is, I would've liked it. But now it's too late."

Jim made do by orchestrating the choir at Holy Trinity Greek Orthodox Church, at 12th and Guthrie, in the neighborhood on a rise between downtown and the river, where the well-kept homes still house much of Tulsa's Greek population, one of the city's earliest migrations.

iii. A Nathan of Millions

Come to America and you cook for Americans. Whatever tradition you import becomes, in time, a gray component of the melting pot. In time, the line between culinary culture and repeat business is crossed and the dish compromises its authenticity, the thing that gave it meaning. Sometimes, it disappears altogether, and forever.

By the time Nathan Handwerker got his hands on the hot dog, it had ceased to be a sausage and become an icon, a tasty symbol of manifest destiny. "All you had was the hot dog," Jim explains it. "You didn't need a plate, you could carry it with you. It was all there—wiener and bun—everything on the go."

In 1919, three years after Handwerker, a Pole, founded Nathan's on Coney Island, Christ Economou got a call from a few compatriots. "They said to him," the son recalls, " 'We think we found a good concept.' What they'd found was Nathan's."

A young Christ, not long off the boat, went on an American tour in search of restaurants—or, really, shells of old diners abandoned during the war. "They started in McKeesport, Pennsylvania," Jim says, "depending on who you ask." (Some family members say Omaha. That family runs the Coney-I-Lander shop on 41st Street near the Barnes & Noble.) "They went around finding closed-up spaces then bought them for $3000, with the idea that they'd work them for six months and sell them for $6000."

"Ladies Invited" reads a sign in a photo of the McKeesport store that hangs in Jim's shop, on a column behind the Frito Lay rack.

After eating, diners would drink from a communal tin cup floating in a tub of ice water. Like all the stores, it was outfitted with a hot dog grill, two steamers—one for buns, the other for chili—and enough product to open the doors.

"You see, they came here with the idea that they had to make money. Not to become rich, that was never the point. They had to make enough money for the families back home. First, all the sisters, then for the other women in the village. They did this even up to the late 1960s. They'd pay for the pipes, so they could run water to the village. Things not done by the municipality."

Agrafa is the name for a nameless place. At one point, I ask Jim something insane like, "Where did it all begin?" and he says, "You have to go back to the village." The village is somewhere in Agrafa, Greek for "not written." Agrafa is a rugged terroir, with a people and custom to match. Ironically, it was Agrafa's monasteries that preserved the Greek language during 400 years of Ottoman occupation.

Christ left Agrafa for America in order to find five dowries for his sisters. "There was no other way. He couldn't break into a business. In Athens, you had to grease too many palms."

McDonald's Greece opened its first restaurant in 1991, in Syntagma Square. Jim smiles at how much it must have cost them. Today in Greece, there are 48 McDonald's shops employing 1,500 Greeks.

Crescendo

Bill Klentos and Jim Pinos, the Greeks of Mecca Coffee Company, sold a lot of goods in their Boulder Avenue shop: olives, cheeses, spices, teas. But coffee took the cake.

"They would come to church with it in their clothes," Jim recalls. "They never got it out and you could smell it on them ... the heavenly smell of coffee."

Before the downtown exodus, Mecca and Coney Island were neighbors, the wiener shop adjacent to the newspaper building and Mecca a block north. Like most eateries at the time, Mecca had a famous chili recipe. Though Ike's, around the corner, set the standard.

"We shared an alley," Jim says. "Our back door and their back door opened up across from each other. During breaks, our cooks and their cooks shared drinks, cigarettes." He smiles. "Trade secrets."

Ike's coveted recipe, like black-market gold, must have bought a lot of drinks. After all, a coney without a chili is a mere dog. "This entire operation," Jim confesses, "revolves around chili."

Today, the cheese is now cheesefood and the chili taken for granted. Mecca, now in Brookside, still blends coffees, if not to order. For Jim, it isn't the same.

"I would like to have 30 percent Arabic, 30 percent African, some Columbian and so on. And they would blend it and cook it for you. You have to blend. The African has such great aroma, but not a lot of body. So you need Columbian. For me, I have to have that aroma.

"Today, you find a brand to go with and that's that. It's dumbed down, like everything."

iv. Christ the Complex

At 21, Christ Economou came to America with $21 to his name. He was told not to accept less than a dollar a day wages. "People came up to him," Jim says, "right off the boat: 'Eighty cents! Eighty cents!' He said no thank you. From the first day he arrived, they came offering jobs."

He finally got that dollar a day, driving railroad spikes across the continent—starting in Wisconsin and moving west. Working the conveyor in that Sheboygan slaughterhouse, he saw a human hand float down the belt. Sheboygan comes from the Chippewa but its meaning meanders. Excerpts from a 1920 city directory:

> The word or sentence expresses a tradition that a great noise, coming underground from the region of Lake Superior, was heard at this river. (Others) agree that Sheboygan is derived from *jibaigan*, meaning any perforated object. One authority claims the Indian word meant "send through."

A current chamber of commerce web site prefers "passage of

waterway between the lakes." Wistful for conventions now ignored, and with an almond's trace of bitterness, Jim embraces the "perforated object" translation.

"In the earlier days," he says nostalgically, "unions played a big role in taking care of people."

The Agrafiotes who became disciples of Nathan's, intent on spreading word of the hot dog, saved Christ from the abattoir and began the mission, starting in McKeesport and moving south. [Chili, a gospel unto its own, is an addition of bastardly conception. Detroit is widely credited with smothering a hot dog in chili sauce, so perhaps the Greeks grabbed it there, on their way out of Wisconsin. Cincinnati, for the record, claims to have first put spaghetti into chili and beans to concoct the storied "three-way." Nathan's menu today offers a coney "topped with our special mild chili with beans".]

Christ and company opened six stores in Texas and then came north. He launched a legacy with Coney Island Hot Weiner Shop yet gave his heart and soul to another. Long on vision but short on eyesight, Christ quit globetrotting and answered a more ancient calling. It had been building in him since the village.

All but blind at the age of 9, he was sitting in the congregation one day, dead to the world. "The village priest came down the aisle," Jim says, "and grabbed him by the ear, this blind boy, and said, 'From now on, this is your position,' and he pointed to a place near the altar.

"And he stayed right there for 74 years."

"It's always in the front of my mind," said the renowned cantor Hazzan Alberto Mizrahi, "that when I sing Jewish music and hazzanut (a Jewish cantorial tradition), whether on the pulpit or the stage, not only am I preserving the music, but I'm affirming the existence of the Jewish people and the culture that was doomed."

In canting, Christ had conquered. "He loved the church here, the people. He told his partners they could do what they wanted, but he was staying. Ultimately, they went back to Greece."

Diminuendo

In a famous newsreel, Rita Hayworth has come home from somewhere sporting a topcoat. Some European theater, probably.

A reporter sticks a microphone in her face and asks her how it feels to be back in America. She says she just wants to eat a hot dog. As a line, it seems mildly rehearsed yet oddly genuine. "... a hot dog," she says then grins that shit-eating grin of hers. The face that launched a thousand slips. I remember being amazed to learn, whenever I did, that Rita Hayworth was born Margarita Carmen Cansino and was discovered dancing in Mexican nightclubs.

When I was a teen, there was a fad to design flavored snack crackers and then sell them with pretend names. Like Bacon Thins and Chicken in a Biskit. Artificially flavored and preserved for posterity, these things got in my blood. I can still taste them, still can feel the vegetable-fat residue filmy on my fingertips. They are the original bad taste in my mouth. Only, they tasted good. The flavor they imparted will never leave me, like a chip implanted with all the taste-bud data one might ever need. I could have been a Nabisco poster child, so hungry was I for TVP. I was the target market and they sunk the arrow in so deep that I just left it there, snapping the shaft off at the skin and resigning myself to the barbs buried in the flesh.

CHAPTER IV

MY MOTHER IS A CHICKEN

My mother's brothers married odd birds. Frances was a wild-eyed zany with a voice like a trapped cat and a way of haranguing young boys that kept me on edge. She stood tall and broad, like a dark, autumn oak, all limbs and dry leaves.

"Duck," real name of Ida Mae, spoke softly, kept a shiny kitchen of fluorescent lighting and tight linoleum. Duck stuck close to the ground, ruffled few feathers, seldom rattled the cage.

And Nita, Hack's wife, the one he brought back from Germany along with the contraband sword he tucked away in blue velvet. Nita would juggle oranges against the living room wall, would wail at our dour young faces, and sob wildly at things that barely warranted attention. The family smiled at her in jubilant horror, as we might have ironic images of the war from which she'd eloped.

All our people fried chicken, not all of them well, but all of them good people.

Frances tended to burn hers at the edges, I think through a

combination of fear—of the undone breast and its buried tender—and considerable loathing. By the look on her face, she couldn't have much enjoyed cooking. The table she set for us, laid out with something less than aplomb, creaked from heavy bowls of limp beans, soggy fried potatoes, and beaten-down squash, not to mention the main event, the oil-charred chicken with the mealy exterior tasting of paste and carbon. Crust it never had a chance to be.

Not long after Howard, her husband and Barney's eldest, died, Frances returned to her native West Virginia. Poor Frances, screaming at her boy, my pale cousin Mickey of the slamming screen door, the junkyard of Hot Wheels, the folded poster of Raquel Welch circa *One Million Years* B.C. Mick was among the impediments to her setting a good spread.

Duck's husband, Charles, is Barney's youngest son. He farmed turkeys, raising them in twin pens, until Cargill and others altered that landscape. Hack, born Haskell, died in Killeen, Texas, home of Fort Hood. We visited them once, watched the veterans drink beer in a VFW hall, slipping quarters into a dated jukebox.

My mother, Bonna, moved to Tulsa. Her sister, Mary, to Alaska, Puerto Rico, and other military bases before coming home.

The land of all their upbringing is steeped in fertility, flanked by branches of the Canadian River, whose waters percolate beneath rows of corn, peanut plants and cow ponds full of frying fish that compete for table space with banty roosters.

The land of my mother's family triangulated Pittsburg County, from Scipio in the north to Savanna in the South, then east to Hartshorne. A land of imprisonment for some—in the shadow of the state penitentiary at McAlester—and opportunity for others. A land of milk and honey, of sorghum and sow. And of fowl.

In 1911, William Procter and James Gamble outsmarted lard and came up with white gold. Crisco, "the first solidified shortening product made entirely of vegetable oil, was the result of hydrogenation, a new process that produced shortening that would stay in solid form year-round, regardless of temperature," reads the Web site. Crisco and bacon drippings both, say Cheryl Alters Jamison and Bill Jamison in *Texas Home Cooking*, are indispensable to creating a recipe of "East Texas Fried Chicken." Bacon drippings being a kissing cousin of lard.

Barnett Asbury Poole entered this land from Lockesburg, Arkansas, near DeQueen in 1928. It was not a clean break. For years afterward, Faunds Pool (Barney seems to have added the "E") and another of his sons, Carl and/or Norman, would make the drive from Lockesburg to Barney's place west of McAlester.

"They'd pull up into the drive and fall out of the car just drunk," my mother told me. "The Cobb side of the family was quiet. But that Poole side, they enjoyed life."

Barney took no pleasure from a cup, none that I ever saw. He had only a taste for his plug tobacco. And for all the fat of the land: fruit laid up in cans, mealy fish fries, pan gravies, and smokehouse bacons. Chickens roamed his yard, pecking head down until wrung not by Barney but by Ella, his first of three brides.

"Oh, two or three times a week, at least," my mother recalled. They ate roosters, the smaller the better.

Ella would open the gate of the coop, wielding a homemade rod of thin, sturdy wire with a hook curled manually into the tip of it. With a darting flick of the wrist she'd ankle the rooster and, with her free hand, latch onto his neck. Then a sure and sturdy twist, a draining of the geekish blood, and a long, arduous plucking.

"And when she got to the pinfeathers, she'd burn those off with a match," my mom recalled. "Then, she'd give that chicken a good scaldin'." By this, my mother means a ferocious hot water bath in a deep, clean sink.

Frying chicken, I have learned the hard way, is not a birthright. The technique, unlike the chin, does not seem to have been passed down. Much as I attempt to channel the innate touch—what the apostle Paul called that knowledge which passes all understanding—my effort fails to produce the kind of success I have tasted time and again at the Poole Tables, memorably at his but more often at my mother's.

What I picture as I dredge the pieces of thigh and breast for a bath in hot oil is two kitchens: My mother's, which over the years was really three kitchens that have somehow become one through the act of cooking and the art of consistency. Three stovetops each within five miles of one another as we moved from Sheridan Terrace onto Shadow Mountain and beyond.

As I said, two kitchens: my mother's, one, and her momma's and daddy's, two.

Hers was a cook's kitchen, hectic at the holidays but busy anytime, echoing the sounds of a southern-bred cook, and each sound accompanied by its own signature smell. I reserve the more ethereal "aroma" for air fresheners. A kitchen like ours produced smells. Besides, in my mother's house, we ate aromatics—chunks of carrots and onions, and celery studding chunky beef stews—rather than simply flavoring stock with them. Southern cooks do not coerce carrots, they cook and eat them. Garlic, that most aromatic of all, did not find fashion in my mouth until I began to feed myself, picking it up in books and spreading it all through the house, or houses, generally.

I understand that fried chicken requires a tight, crisp crust—an alchemy of oil and flour and skin—insulating a moist, meaty flesh, and that a perfectly fried breast might look like a fly ball wedged into an oily brown mitt. But I see it better than I cook it.

I stare into the skillet and its roiling oil in the moment before I test its readiness with a pinch of flour. You can peer deeply into a blackened skillet of hot fat, into an almost bottomless pit, as I imagine LaBrea to be, or hell and its cauldron of souls. I hold the breaded meat over the oil and guide it into the skillet delicately, like a sapper anticipating an explosion. Then I watch, and the longer and deeper I peer the more hypnotized I become, until I succumb to a paralyzing trance during which time I am able to conjure things past, present, and incidental. Mere seconds pass, but they represent the tainted hours and lost years spent over skillets and sinks and near empty bottles of wine in an attempt to get chicken right.

Proust needed a tea cake to find his way back in time but that is too dainty for me.

Anymore, fried chicken is likely to mean boneless convenience-store tenders draining on paper towels set beneath the orange glow of hood warmers. Their bonelessness I take as a testament to commerce and culinary climes. It is a noxious fume, that of stale ClearFry being ventilated into a parking lot heavy with the metallic tinge of gas being pumped.

Though tenders make tidy road food, fried chicken down on the farm still veers toward the basic eight-piece ensemble, bones attached. It survives relatively unscathed in this Oklahoma of vanishing youth and diminishing wealth, where methheads and Methodists populate the hamlet's lone diner to down cups of bottomless coffee for a buck.

When folks die, we fry. Fried chicken offers crunchy respite at the alcohol-free wakes of Red Bed Plains tradition, sitting up brown and strong in a wide sea of soft, spoonable dishes. The strength of such ritual is enough to fortify an entire host of family and friends, and offers comfort amid the silent pining. The sag on the funeral table is formidable, and one is tempted to trace fried chicken and all its trimmings back to the feasts of early saints, their disciples and lesser followers clinging to hope at the end of a drumstick sticky with fried skin, the salt stabilizing the unsure earth, the pepper providing a speck of savory irony.

A chicken, fit to be fried, is a delicious martyr.

In its entirety, Fried Chicken a la Rufus Estes, from *Good Things to Eat as Suggested by Rufus*, looks like this: Cut up two chickens. Put a quarter a pound of butter, mixed with a spoonful of flour, into a saucepan with pepper, salt, little vinegar, parsley, green onions, carrots, and turnips, and heat. Steep the chicken in this marinade three hours, having dried the pieces and floured them. Fry a good brown. Garnish with fried parsley.

My own fried chicken looks right enough but lacks depth. I think I cook it too fast and furiously. I once tried frying it in two inches of oil and spent an entire roll of paper towels mopping up my mistake. When I fry it now, I set up a cordon.

My mother will fry chicken whenever I ask her, and I know not to push it. Chicken in her hands has a flavor that is hers and hers alone, as if my mother were a chicken in a past life, scratching her way across the coop yard, her proud breast thrust out, the gentle folds of her neck wagging in the strut, her tail feathers flagging the lone, lucky cock o' the walk, and her legs—meaty at the joint, sinewy and strong as they taper to earth—provoking the farmer's wife to her dutiful wring and pluck.

Fried chicken is soul food and so you'll find it in riches the further southeast you go. In Oklahoma, it survives as the stepchild of culinary displacement. Lacking a food of our own, we adopt fried chicken.

The South has a soul, but Oklahoma has no soul. A soul needs a closet where old ghosts can steep and ripen, and the plains of Oklahoma are too outback for that. In the days of Depression and dust, Oklahoma lost a good many of its sons and daughters to diaspora, the winds of despair spreading the Okies west, their distended bellies swelling in the fertile valley.

What remains of Oklahoma, in lieu of a soul, is a stamina, a legacy of waiting and weathering. Storms swirl around us, natives and settlers alike, and we accept them as part of our condition. We are conditioned by them, be they tortured cycles of endemic poverty, marital hit-and-miss, or tornadoes that roar out of desolate Texas each spring. The twisters scoot into the trough of Oklahoma and lay waste before moving on.

Sometime in the last couple of decades, the diner's appetite for legs and wings dwindled, with wings going mostly to Buffalo and legs reserved for restaurant logos. Our taste for dark meat was consumed by the newfangled breast. The "pick of the chick" became a boneless breast. Grilled.

Sometime in the '70s, the chicken sandwich straddled up next to the burger and took a heavy chunk out of the fried chicken market. The boneless breast ushered in the Reagan era, with its Hollywood health-consciousness and retraction of anything traditional. "Fried" became the riot act of the dietary witch trials, skin stripped off before the flesh hit the fire. Bones dismissed in the drawing and quartering never made the pyre. Fake breasts—on a woman or a soft white bun—set the new standard of living and dining. "Rubber tits," I've heard them called, those boneless, sauced chicken slabs fed to us at awards ceremonies and charity benefits.

Barney died before his old Arkansas became the front of the boneless assault. Pork was yet to seize on the genius of being second, so chicken had the white meat market to itself. Back then, when you stopped at the AQ Chicken House in Springdale, you stopped for a fried chicken dinner whatever the hour. Today, sandwiches take up a full page of the menu. Fried as a hallmark has all but died.

Nor had the captains of industry emerged. Don Tyson was yet to have a president's ear. Bo Pilgrim, the pride of Pittsburg (this one in Texas) even in bankruptcy, had yet to erect his 20,000-square foot "Cluckingham Palace," a monument to all things without a backbone. A chicken was still a bird, with a beak. It was covered in feathers, not plastic. It did not look like an air-hockey puck.

It still had pluck.

Fried chicken finds a way. Like the stones that crop up all over Ireland no matter how deep and often the farmer digs, fried chicken surfaces inevitably on the menus of southern restaurants with any measurable staying power. In a migrant town called Krebs, near McAlester in Oklahoma, it found an unlikely home alongside mom-and-pop marinara.

McAlester is named for J.J. McAlester, a man who built his mansion mining coal. Charles Portis saw fit to write him into *True Grit*, so formidable was he. While J.J. built the house, Italian labor built the legacy. They also built Krebs, a tiny hamlet best known for its eateries, of which Giacomo's, Roseanna's, Isle of Capri, and Pete's Place remain.

Any roadside restaurant in rural Oklahoma that isn't paying its rent by Tex-Mex or buffet Mandarin knows the one-two-three punch of "Steaks-Chicken-Seafood." At such a place, the steak will be serviceable and perhaps even delicious. The seafood is more than likely fried shrimp. Which leaves chicken, fried of course, and this is always the safest bet. Enterprising menus will even fry up the livers (an order will include at least a dozen).

On Pete's menu, below lamb fries,[1] is "Italian Fried Chicken." Unchanged over several decades, it's Italian in that Italians cooked

---

1 First item on Pete's online menu is a $25 plate of sheep's testicles, fried in cracker crumbs and garnished with lemon wedges. Only three items—all of them steaks, and one of them a 30-ounce sirloin for two—price higher. "Slices of Lamb from Iceland" they are described, though they are as likely to come from New Zealand, in a box, from a cooperative. And based on the size—akin to one of the Silly Putty eggs—"sheep fries" is a much more apt, if less delicate, description.

it. The grandsons and great grandsons of Pietro Piegari, that is, with the legacy losing face as the years pass, the genes recede and the lore mutates.

Consistency at a KFC is a matter of science and strategy, organized and designed in some home office to allow a moderately trained line cook the least possible margin for error, which anymore must be and practically is zero. The Colonel fries more chicken for charity than my mother did during my tenure in her nest.

I'd say once a month, tops, or 10 times a year. Times 18 years to arrive at less than 200 fries—200 or so chances in a lifetime to hone the art of the scald. In my mom's kitchen, weeks passed between each order, time enough it could be reasoned for the subtleties of the cook's craft to lose footing. You can cook anything decently on the first try if your heart's in it and you source with care. But we're talking fried chicken, not an easy flavor to send into orbit, however easy it might be to reach a state of readiness.

Cook anything 200 times and you should arrive at some kind of standard. But it isn't the fried chicken I ate on the way out my mother's door that I recall; rather, the brown birds of the wonder years, peaking at the height of adolescence, for me around 1977, the year we lost Presley—a fine fried chicken eater if ever a cock walked.

The problem with recipes is that you feel as though you have to follow them, and them is usually a list of specific ingredients and a series of steps. Stray from them at your own peril. My mother's method for chicken does not require a recipe because, one, she has cooked it many times and, two, it really is quite simple. For a curious son, achingly so.

I hate to write it down now, when it's remained silent all these years, but in lieu of frying decent chicken this is what I do. I write shit down. I call it "Ella's and Bonna's Fried Chicken" and it goes not something but precisely like this:

Cut up as small a chicken as you can find into several pieces. If the breasts are too large, cut them each in half. When you are ready to fry, rinse and pat dry the chicken and season lightly but thoroughly with salt and pepper. Season a deep dish of Gold Medal All-Purpose flour with more salt and pepper. Season it generally, imagining the 10 chicken pieces as you do so. Dredge the chicken in the flour and set aside on a fresh plate while you bring to hot a well-seasoned, cast-iron skillet of Crisco shortening. Check the oil for heat by dropping in a pinch of flour. (If it sizzles at all, the oil is ready.) When the oil is hot, re-dredge each piece in the seasoned flour—by now, the first coat will have absorbed and made a kind of wet paste applicant—and set gently into the skillet, skin-side down. Fry until the oil begins to crackle and then lower the heat a bit. Listen for a steady but firm sound, as you don't want the oil too wild at this point. Cook until the underside begins to brown, sear, and appear cooked, then flip it and cook a few more minutes until you have an even browning of the skin. Once this is achieved, pull the chicken from the pan with a set of tongs and drain on a plate lined with paper towels. Stick the chicken in a warm oven until ready to serve. It can rest there for up to two hours without losing its moisture or crispiness.

I like my chicken, like myself, with the bones intact. Bones are evidence of life and it's life, after all, that flavors a living thing. Meat hanging to bones is evidence of some plan, a design rendered by something beyond man to give him character and architecture. When I chew against a leg, thigh, or breast bone to extract the last of the meat (each piece demanding a slightly different approach, be it a joint or a rib cage), I push into the bone confident that it will push back. Bones give my teeth reason for being, gnawing, pressing reasons, and without them—bones, I mean—who knows how long before my teeth fall out of my head from all the boneless mush I am left to chew.

I have Barney to thank for all the lead and gold in my head, if my mother is to be believed. "You got your mom's chalky teeth," she'll say, and if I got it from her then she got it from him. Or from the woman he married. In truth, I could blame my grandmother on my cavities, on the pains that dart through my molars when I segue between hot and cold, but I never met this Ella. And even if it was her side, the Cobb side, that laid the DNA for my slow decay, Barney married into it and so the case rests with him, somewhere in a field on Tannehill Road not a mile off U.S. 75, with the 11-story Hotel Aldridge and the dilapidated state prison lording over the Canadian River valley flats.

Is it popcorn you taste, or movie theaters? A hot dog, or night baseball in some bush-league park? Peanuts, or a well-tended bar that allows you to litter its floors in spent shells? When you taste cheddar, is it nachos you're tasting, or England? What is coffee but a late-night reminder, a roasted bean, an off-taste in the mouth between sweet kisses? Orange peel can be a car freshener, a cocktail, or one of those soft candies that used to appear around the holidays. Anymore, it means Pei Wei, which uses it to flavor a Mongolian beef, which no doubt tastes nothing like Mongolia. A Budweiser tastes of college, a lemon of vomit, and water—allegedly tasteless—tastes to me of waste and politics. But that's Tulsa water.

CHAPTER V

CORN

Jaywalking near my downtown office building one morning, I nearly stepped in the middle of a flattened pigeon. A paste of damp blood and pulp affixed it to the asphalt. A hot wind ruffled the lifeless, flightless feathers. I didn't stare, just glanced, but the gape was wide and nothing hidden. I turned away from something green that could have been an olive, and I wouldn't write it off. An olive, or maybe an organ. A heart. Bird innards, torn up, make a rotten fruit soup: black plums, blue cherries, and gray grapes, set in blood syrup. Unmistakable, amid the purée of flesh and blood and bone, shone an undigested corn kernel. A diamond in the rough.

I was borne of corn. My mother grew womanly on the milk and meat of cows and pigs that ate raw corn. Her cheeks, plump and shiny, nearly burst with the syrup and starch of stored corn. She'd saturate her raw, farmgirl's hands in the famed Corn Husker's Lotion.

On the midway of the Tulsa State Fair, my dad would fall for the boiled ear of corn on a stick. He'd lather it in butter and season it liberally with salt and pepper, the way he dusted everything savory that he ate. Dizzy from rides and cotton candy, we watched him pile it on.

"Pepper!" said my friend and rival from five houses down. "Nobody dumps pepper on their corn-on-the-cob."

"Oh, yeah?" my dad said between bites.

I was no riper than nine, prone to collusion and treachery. Did I side with my friend, feign shame and further heap humiliation upon my father, in order to show solidarity and save face? The other way—the way it went—is that I took in the corn-eating scene beneath the night glow of autumn amusements and felt pity for my dad being scorned. He ate, obliviously, and my loyalty to him grew with each disappearing row of kernels.

Soon after, "Because of my teeth," he argued, my dad took to carving his corn from the cob, and sprinkled on more salt and pepper than ever.

Corn was gold in the great city of Tenochtitlán, the city of the Toltec before the Aztec, then of the Mexica (Me-sheek-a), Mexico City, city of corn gardens situated atop twin mountains, amid great lakes. Corn came up in chinampas, "floating gardens," in four quarters of the city, a land tilled communally by 750,000 farmers, or three-fourths of the citizenry. Human dung fed the mounds, which were irrigated by dams, dykes, canals and aqueducts—a master plan that channeled annual flooding.

How important was this corn? Taxes came in the form of it: "one large mantle, four small ones, a basket of shelled maize, and 100 cobs." How dear? The famine of 1450 set the limit, with families selling offspring for baskets of corn, 400 cobs for a girl, 500 for a boy.

For ancient cultures wedded to it, corn predates memory. It is the nut where history and myth meet, like starch and sugar, never again to solely be. In times and terms of war, corn fortified the young soldiers and deified the early martyrs. "Maize gods native to Central and South America," writes Betty Fussell in *The Story of Corn*, "were far more ancient than Christian saints or the crucified God whose image the Spaniards planted in maize fields red with the blood of conquest."

When the Maya wrote their book, corn took root at the corpus of humanity: "And here is the beginning of the conception of humans, and of the search for the ingredients of the human body. Said the Sovereign Plumed Serpent: 'Morning has come for humankind, for the people of the face of the earth.' "

In Maya consciousness, corn and water are the body and blood. "After that," the narration goes, "they put it into words:

> the making, the modeling of our first mother-father,
> with yellow corn, white corn alone for the flesh,
> food alone for the human legs and arms,
> for our first fathers, the four human works.
> It was staples alone that made up their flesh."

In his history of Spanish conquest, Father Bernardino de Sahagún, plumbing the remnants of Aztec belief, rhapsodized the native corn growers:

"The good farmer, the field worker, is active, agile, diligent, industrious: a man careful of things, dedicated—dedicated to separate things. [He goes] without his sleep, without his food; he keeps vigil at night, his heart breaks.

"The bad farmer is a shirker, a lukewarm worker."

Sahagún was beside himself. The goddess of maize, Chicome Couatl, and Cinteotl, the god of ripe corn, became his adopted spirits. It had happened before: The Aztecs, and the Maya who preceded them, absorbed the deities of storied cultures whose origins were the very mesh of corn, sun, and rain.

When my mom's dad took us fishing, we used as live a bait as was possible. For mere perch, it was freshly dug earthworms ("night crawlers," my grandfather called them, filling his Folgers can); newly minted minnows for crappie; and strong, twisting "shiners" (just bigger minnows) for the coveted black bass. For catfish, we employed a ruse decayed, sloppy, and unspeakable, which says a little about us and a lot about a catfish. "Channel cat," we called them, denoting the variety but, as well, establishing a vernacular.

Such was fishing in the country, on the pitched banks of the muddy Wild Horse. But in the city, in a pond at the end of the block, in a field that separated the two editions of Sheridan and Magnolia Terrace if not for long, we baited our hooks with corn. Several of us would line the stone and mud banks and toss our lines into the civic muck. We'd study each other cautiously, angling for the good water, waging war on perch and each other. "I got a nibble," you'd hear. A nibble on a Green Giant Niblet.

We caught stunted perch of a green-yellow jaundice, when we caught them. Often, their lips would have missed the corn, pushed it up onto the shaft of the hook, where it clung just off the fish's bony lip, taunting the silver-and-black bead of fisheye.

"Corn may be eaten from the cob," announced Frederick Stokes in *Good Form: Dinners Ceremonious and Unceremonious* (1890). "Etiquette permits this method, but does not allow one to butter the entire length of an ear of corn and then gnaw it from end to end. ... Good form disallows it." Poor Stokes would have had a field day with my dad's Uncle Rocky. Dining at our table during one of his rare trips to town, Rocky broke all the rules by engaging in hand-to-hand combat with a full cob of corn. Not only did he butter the bursting, beautiful length of it, he laid waste to the golden rod in a one-off in which he barely took breath. Rocky ripped, the kernels misting sweet starch, stray germs and husks anointing his chin, his cheeks, his upper lip, most of his placemat. After one cob had been dispensed with, the great Roscoe Kinsey would tell tales of his time as sheriff in an Arizona town, sell spin of great pranks he'd pulled and great fish he'd lured and landed, and level jokes about anything at all, just to hold our gaze. "Bullshit artist," my cousin would say.

Rocky's sister, my grandmother, sat back and smiled timidly. Jewell, less rambunctious with her corn, preferred it from the can, where the sweetness fermented on a stale note and no grassy corn gluten survived processing. Jewell's corn, canned corn, stuck to nobody's face and went well with stringy roast beef cut errantly with versus elegantly across the well-done grain. Digestion here was hard-won. After such a meal, I'd find bits of that canned corn glowing back up at me from the bathroom bowl, as yellow and wholesome as ever.

My father-in-law grows a bit of corn, in a patch no wider than a back patio. What they don't eat, and what ears the animals and rain don't take, he saves for us.[1] You can be convinced, upon eating three-day-old corn, that sweetness is relative. But, really, it's only fleeting.

Cooking time depends entirely upon starch content. Therefore, taste a few kernels from the tip to test sweetness. Sweeter hybrids eat well raw. Take care: Starchier corns go tough when they go. Cook quickly and taste — cook one ear as a test case. As for time, err on the side of less.

Behold corn, beans, and squash, the "Oklahoma vegetable triad." You learn that in Maurice Goff's Oklahoma History, eigth grade, Thoreau Junior High. "Corn, beans, and sqwarsh," he said it, like we owned it. Succotash (from the Narragansett m'sickquatash) was simply an offshoot of the planting, beans being allowed to climb up corn stalks in the Indian garden. Early "dumplings" of new corn and young beans wrapped in corn leaves are a far cry from the masa-and-pulled-pork tamales that one native cook I know insists be steamed for precisely one hour. Far ... yet not.

"How to Make Succotash," from *Western Farmer and Gardener*:

To about half a pound of salt pork, add 3 quarts of cold water, and set it to boil. Now cut off 3 quarts of green corn from the cobs; set the corn aside, and put the cobs to boil with the pork, as they will add much to the richness of the mixture. When the pork has boiled, say half an hour, remove the cobs and put in 1 quart of freshly-gathered beans, green, shelled beans; boil again for fifteen minutes; then add 3 quarts of corn and let it boil another fifteen minutes.

In Tehran, street vendors serve balal—brined, fresh corn cooked over hot coals. In Alexandria, they call it durra, and the air in the market stalls reeks with the caramelized aroma. We still grow the bulk of the world's corn, but China is closing the gap.

Of an enticing 250, a mere three recipes for corn—and none

1 "Eat 'em now," Father John warns. "They won't be any good after that!" Indeed, corn sugar begins the inevitable march to starch the moment it's off the stalk, the sweetness slipping like silk in the night. "Make sure to have as little distance as possible between the corn patch and the kettle," instructs John Doerper in *Eating Well* (Pacific Search Press, 1984).

of them very convincing—are printed in Barrenechea's quite beautiful and informative *The Cuisines of Spain*. All three are of Canarian influence: Traders en route to the Americas (and back) would first pull into the Canary Islands, of course, before hitting the mainland. Corn, it appears, failed to pass through Gibraltar with any muster.

That the cornmeal mush of the colonial hearth would live again in this neo-culinary America as polenta speaks to the persistence of corn. Polenta is a storied dish, though, made first with wheat—the Romans, and perhaps Etruscans, made a gruel called pulmentum—and adapted to corn via import. And while your sautéed pork chop with pan glaze is likely to sit smack in a dab of creamy polenta, nobody paints like the Italians, whose art with the polenta form plateaus with the northern dish called polenta coi osei: "It consists of tiny songbirds, spit-roasted, each wrapped in a band of fat for cooking," reports Waverly Root in his encyclopedic take on culinary Italy. "Sometimes they are brought to the table with each bird separately bedded on its own slab of polenta moistened with the carefully caught cooking juices."

Thoreau, on Walden, made his own bread, first of "Indian meal" and only later of flour. Preferring the former, Thoreau settled on a loaf of rye and cornmeal. Sometimes, he'd not waste time with the milling and baking. "And pray," he wrote, "what more can a reasonable man desire, in peaceful times, in ordinary noons, than a sufficient number of ears of green sweet-corn boiled, with the addition of salt?"

Sitting on the window ledge at Thoreau Junior High, in the twilight of a spring dance, my drinking buddy Todd reached down and yanked a large stalk of grass from the landscaping, handed it to me and, invoking a popular television commercial of the day, said straight-faced: "You call it corn ... We call it maize."

We howled, secretly tipsy from a quart of Coors that we'd conned a young woman into buying for us at the nearby Git-N-Go as we hid in the asphalt shadows. We were still laughing when they filed out of the dance, and we watched them from our concrete perch—all the curious, starched-shirt boys, and all the gorgeous, corn-fed girls.

Jeff, from the neighborhood, rode a Yamaha, played defensive tackle and beat me to a mustache by mere weeks. He and I and a woman named Dulce for whom Jeff worked used to sit around for hours eating a dip made of melted cheese and canned mushrooms, ladling it with the big, flat Fritos, and washing it down with Little Kings Cream Ale. It felt wondrous, driving all the way from our houses on the city's then-southern edge to Dulce's guest house over behind a private school in the heart of old Tulsa. There are but two ingredients in Fritos: corn and salt. It seems as if there should be more.

Once, I gave Jeff four dollars and he gave it, and four more, to his brother Kevin and, shazam, we got two six-packs of liquor-store Michelob out of it. Jeff outweighed me plenty, but I giddily kept pace. That night, I woke up on his bathroom floor, having horked into the bowl and never gotten up. Earlier in the evening, halfway into the six, I began to taste in my drying mouth the unmistakable and ever-pleasant warmth of corn. Later, when somebody gave me a clandestine can of Pearl in the school parking lot, I noticed it even more.

It was transplanted Scots who distilled the first drams of bourbon in Bourbon County, Kentucky. Elijah Craig, a country Baptist, used his limestone-filtered waters to dunk sinners and distill spirit. For corn liquor to be called bourbon, by law it must contain 51 percent of the grain. Traditionally, Peruvian brewmeisters (women, always) would spit into a corn mash, thus providing the enzymatic starter for the native beer, chicha.

Used to be we ate Kellog's Corn Flakes, spooning on the sugar, so much that it would gather in the bowels of the milky bowl like gray silt in a chalk pond. Soon I switched to Sugar Pops—later renamed, for transparency's sake, to Corn Pops and, now, just Pops—but moved on to Sugar Crisps after eating an entire box of Pops and vomiting the corn-coated lot of it into the kitchen sink. Then came Corn Chex, born of Rice Chex, which begat Wheat Chex, as I worked my way through the entire Chex family line.

I accompanied my mother to her grocer's one Saturday and convinced her to buy me a brand of bagged popcorn that caught my eye. Normally, she made our popcorn from relative scratch. When I got it home, I ripped open the bag and, probably in front of *Dark Shadows* or *The Green Hornet*, ate the entire bag. I threw it up, too.

After liking it at first, I soon learned to pass on helpings of creamed corn.

Arguments have been made that corn is not a grain at all, but a fruit, the germ of which resides inside nutrient flesh. Corn converts its sugar to starch, versus the other way around. All the oil, by the way, is in the germ. My wife nibbles corn twice; once to get the hull and bulk of the kernel, then again to salvage the germ. I try to watch her teeth as she performs this dexterity, but the moves are too delicate.

I've long since lost my craving for a candy bar but there was a time we were inseparable. You name it—Snickers, Milky Way, Mr. Goodbar, Crackle, Hershey's, Almond Joy, Reese's, Zero, Zagnut, Butterfinger, Three Musketeers, Payday, Nestlés Crunch, O Henry ,and Heath—I segued among them shamelessly, rapaciously. I was young, fairly firm of tooth and full of vigor, and the sugar may have rotted my mouth but it helped sustain me in my youth. Somewhere, sometime, though, a good many of the bars fell under the spell of high-fructose corn syrup and I became little more than a hog or a heifer, corn-fed and fidgety and suddenly conscious of becoming fat. So don't blame me if I blame the end of innocence on the sudden appropriation of corn syrup for sugar cane.

You have to stand back to take in all of Antonio Gaudí's unfinished Sagrada Familia, city blocks at least. For it did not occur to me standing in, under, adjacent or atop the cathedral that the four spires of la Sagrada are simply four great, towering ears of corn. Stone panels jut beneath coverless windows, designed to funnel the sea breeze of Barcelona.

As with certain hybrid ears, the alternating nubs and holes depict a less-than-wholesome genome. For those who prefer their cathedrals to follow more conventional lines, Gaudí's church is a bum ear of corn. Such is its nature. The towers, which tilt just a little, just enough, are topped ornately: Hosanna y Excelsis, spelled out in colored glass, crowned in a tassel of sun-drenched, daisy-shaped stone.

The latterday preacher Cotton Mather sowed his fields with corn because of its great profundity and adaptability. "What is not useful is vicious," is a Matherism. This copiousness led to wild mutations in the early days of American corn rearing, birthing toothless and cockeyed cobs colored like gila monsters and shaped like raptor toes.

"Because it is a mutant," writes William Woys Weaver, "corn propagated from a small gene pool will undergo inbreeding depression quickly and irreversibly, just as humans do when they breed with close kin." Hence the need to save seed.

"Let us suppose that the lines of the last chapter extend far over these," wrote Frank Hamilton Cushing, earmarking his learnings for future narratives on life and corn. Employed by John Wesley Powell for the Bureau of American Ethnology, Cushing for five years became Zuni. He wrote words as winding and boundless as Zuni cornbread.

"This bowl of slimy breadstuff swelters but does not out-steam the equally generous trencher of stewed meat-joints and toasted hominy ..."

So, the Zuni knew posole. But sheep's pluck?

"Tilted up, over a primitive plate of sandstone ... a spindle of suet and tidbit-stuffed sheep intestines."

Nothing more than a haggis, bound not with oatmeal but cornmeal mush.

Taste is a verb, and a noun twice—that which excites the tongue, and the word that means stylish choices across the board. Unlike the other senses, it has its own subset. Salty is easy. The tongue recoils like a slug and the buds thirsts. Sweet finds the weakest teeth and invades them. Sour, and its kissing cousin, Bitter, both require Salt or Sweet (or both) to give them function if not meaning. Alone, they are hopeless castaways— Ginger minus Mary Ann. Bitter alone is useless. Bitter in a glass of Campari is mellowed by the sweetness of bergamot and orange peel, the latter lending a further bitterness on top. (Campari hosts a very tasteful website. Some might say tasty.) Salty and Sweet are made livelier by accompaniment, but they usually rely and get by on each other. Umami is, in some essence, the other four chewed up, spit out, and re-ingested.

CHAPTER VI

A QUEST FOR CASSOULET

Four respectable butchers shook their jowls at me when I asked each of them for a pound of an all-American commodity.

"Belly? What are you makin', bacon?"

"Why, you're too young to know what to even *do* with a pork belly!"

"Hmm ... How much you need again?"

"They just ain't no demand for it. Now, if you want a tasty steak, you in the right place."

Pork all around me—Da-Glo hams, synthesized chops, Cryovacked ribs—and nary a belly among them. Even if it is about demand, I find it awkward and not a little damning that in the land of a thousand bacons I can't find a fresh belly. Like finding juice but no apple.

Yes, you can make a cassoulet—a kind of pork and beans salute—without a pork belly. You can substitute pork skin, fatback, salt pork, pork rind, and/or rendered pork fat. You have wiggle room when it comes to pork. Less so with the others meats (lambs and ducks and geese and such) if you want to be authentic. The recipe for Languedoc cassoulet is written more by tradition and disposition than on index cards or in stone. Authenticity often takes a back seat to impulse.

"Like bouillabaisse in Marseille," says Paula Wolfert of cassoulet, just winding up, "paella in Spain, chili in Texas, it is a dish for which there are innumerable recipes and about which discussions quickly turn fierce."

From the region of the Cathars, for whom one God was simply insufficient, why not proselytize over pork and beans? A recipe, like any article of faith, commands a certain allegiance. For my part, I'd not travelled the cassoulet road enough (as a cook, anyway) to be second-guessing the road map. Besides, I was already bucking tradition for convenience. Under this shroud, I opted, for the time being, to hold out for a fresh belly.

The recipe in *The Balthazar Cookbook* promised a "delicious" cassoulet in 22 ingredients (half of them spices and aromatics), in steps that filled not quite two pages. Julia Child's formulae, wouldn't you know, measured six pages, 30 ingredients (a dozen of them animal) and required a meat grinder. Wolfert, under pressure, once offered a dumbed-down take, "A Modern Cassoulet With Two Confits," in her book on Mediterranean cooking.

But, trapped in the vortex of factory fowl and commodity beef, two confit was twice what I could muster.

Let's suppose it's possible to be haunted by a dish, across waters, beyond flavor, before pastime. Not haunted in the way you might eat a box of Krispy Kremes and regret it. Haunted, rather, by a dish as entity, borne of memory, place, and components. Food as familiar as a face in a family snapshot. For reasons that bear examination, cassoulet has become a neglected piece of personal history, not stuck in the pages of a warped family album but glowing in a crock slick with the sheen of a few fats. A thing eaten and absorbed, into body and mind.

"Of all the great dishes which French regional cookery has produced," wrote British cookery writer Elizabeth David, "the cassoulet is perhaps the most typical of true country food, the genuine, abundant, earthy, richly flavoured and patiently simmered dish of the ideal farmhouse kitchen."

Ditto that. My first Languedoc cassoulet was a sumptious affair, the creamy white beans bobbing in the melted stew of pork, tomato, sausage and fat, all giving cause for pause prior to partaking, as if amassed. I recall my first plate of Van Camp's pork and beans with equal clarity: the lone square of soft salt pork hiding among the bland, orange beans. Or was it my hundred and first? I hope it comes as no surprise that both cassoulets, however incomparable, occupy adjacent castles in the appetite of memory.

And the recipe I was about to make, where along the timeline of taste would it eventually fall? Somewhere right of center, I hoped, but I'd resigned myself completely to something well short of sublime. Then why go on with it, right? Clearly, there are more pressing things to do with one's days than rustle up a pork-and-bean casserole. Nostalgia is my lone excuse—the nagging idea of living proof. I was out to resurrect flavor and stir up ghosts. But would my environs hamstring my efforts, or provide a pork barrel? Would a fresh pork belly simply surface, and if it didn't where was I but lost?

"Cassoulet," Waverly Root concluded, "is where you find it."

Thus fortified, I went looking.

Cassoulet emerged from a land steeped in fat and warfare. It is possibly a medieval dish, passed along bloodlines and among vines. Where cassoulet is eaten, red wine is lifeblood.

Three cities—one metropolis, one mecca, one bastion—offer distinct versions of cassoulet. Myriad bastardizations exist, most concocted on the proximity of goods, the tendency of local tongues, the taste of regional cooks. But all tending toward one of the three styles, however loosely, claimed by the three burghs:

Toulouse, Carcassonne, and Castelnaudary are successive stops along the N113 by car, by boat along the Canal du Midi. They form a linear link to this storied crock of the Languedoc, land of the Occitan. All employ a basis of pork: breast, belly, skin, and ubiquitous fats. The distinctions are due to other meats. Toulouse favors an addition of garlicky sausage (its own, of course, for which it is famous), mutton breast, and confit of either duck or goose. The preserved poultry lends a ripe (and necessary, I think) contrast to the flavor of fresh fat. But you're still only two-thirds of the way home, for a cassoulet really is just an occasion to celebrate the plump white bean typically of Tarbais but, it turns out, liable to be from elsewhere.

Carcassonne employs mutton, too, though favors the leg, plus partridges when in season, a historic component that fashion at least discourages. I have eaten five cassoulets, two in the vicinity of Carcassonne, in three seasons, and none of them contained partridge. Nor, for that matter, mutton. Anymore, I have to believe that, unless you stumble upon a rare kitchen, modern cooks of the Midi rely on pork, for its fat and flavor, and preserved duck, for its ubiquity. The majority, I suspect, don't even take the time to make their own confit. And why should they? Vast jars and jugs of it line any supermarket shelf. It would be like asking a pizzeria to cure its own pepperoni.

Castelnaudary, the legendary birthplace of the dish, dominates with pork, everything from cured ham to raw knuckle to fresh loin. But it differs from the other two styles as little or as much as the cook in control desires. Ultimately, the three villes are but signposts en route to the destination that is cassoulet. (Of note: The name comes from the crock in which it cooks—the cassole d'Issel, a town between Castelnaudary and the old market town of Revel.)

At lunch in the Corbières town of Foix, a notorious Cathar stronghold, they seated us on a carpeted terrace that more resembled a tearoom. Fifty feet below flowed the cold, black Ariège. Our friend Stephen—whom we took to calling Etienne after viewing paintings of the saint's stoning, at the hands of the Apostle Paul, no less—our Etienne dined mightily on cassoulet at Foix, while I ate foie gras on toast. Then we hiked up nearby Montsegur in a cold rain, bellies full, imagining the last stand of the legendary sect, done in on this treacherous cliff by siege and rapelling Basque mercenaries. Who fed these fiscal fighters of Cathars, I often wonder, and with what?

The Hotel D'Alibert in Caunes-Minervois makes a mean cassoulet. It is the one I see in dreams. Caunes is an old abbey town, with a passable co-op wine, a deficient bakery, and a cast of characters who make up for it. The South African novelist Christopher Hope sojourns there, so too the Prussian horsetrader named Ditmar that Hope Boswelled in a roman à clef of Languedoc tomfoolery called *Signs of the Heart* (lamentably out of print). There is the bloke Nick, the grand dame Albertina, and the nude-sunbathing Ian. They also are ghosts of a too-fresh past. Their tics and voices torment me now, a land mass removed, and they taunted me there, in our adopted home of Saint-Chinian, one hour east and a mindset removed from the land of Cathars and cassoulets.

Both of my D'Alibert meals were eaten in March, one year apart: A cassoulet eats better in colder weather, it stands to reason, with a large fire in the hearth and a grand plateau of cheese on the end-of-meal horizon. The hotel makes a living off the dish, with the proprietor working his shtick table by table, pouring copious goblets of young wine and squishing about on worn sneakers. Like many Frenchmen, he expresses a fondness for the local cuisine with a calm zeal that exists only in places where tradition and not trend dictates the menu. When I e-mailed him recently to ask of his cassoulet, how it came into being, he replied:

Cher Mark,

Cassoulet,
For the first question, we use a lot of goose fat for the meat.
We use "confit de canard," porc sausage and the porc skin.
For the beans we use lingot from Vendée and they are dry.
And we made always the same.
Best regards.

Frederic

No real surprises, save the Lingot, the Vendée being in the lower Dordogne and nowhere near the Midi. "Made always the same" gave me pause, for I wasn't sure how long d'Alibert had been in business. It wouldn't surprise me to find for centuries. I could only guess at what all else went into Frederic's crock o' beans. He gave me the highlights but not the outline, assuming by my question, I figured, that I knew what I was up against.

Garlic, of course, is elemental. "The soul of Languedoc cooking!" says a gourmand of Castelnaudary. As is a bit of tomato, a few fresh herbs—and a fierce inferno. "Aromatic smells of garlic and herbs escape from the pot as the cassoulet is brought smoking hot from the oven to the table," wrote Elizabeth David. Frederic's D'Alibert crock came blazing from the oven as if kilned there, fats and beans and clay alike.

David takes on cassoulet with nimble clarity. Her ideal dish includes "garlicky pork sausages," "goose drippings or pig's lard," no butter beans ("too floury"), and for the meat to be cut up into "convenient pieces." However English, Liz was no ceremonial prig. Where good food was served, she dug in elbows out. For such a robust offering as cassoulet, she issued a caveat: "Preferably for luncheons when none of the party has anything very active to do afterwards ... Serve on very hot plates, with plenty of young red wine and perhaps a green salad and a good cheese to finish the meal."

"Young" because the wines of the Languedoc are not meant to keep but to drink. Also because what's needed here is less refinement and more raw, acidic whitewashing. The slew of fats in a cassoulet demands a steady freshet in the glass end of things. The redder the better. But how debaucherous of me, putting wine before food.

The beans

I recall being disappointed upon learning that there was no bean native to Oklahoma. Nothing completely our own. Such an odd anamoly for a state of beaneaters. A friend in cassoulet suggested the white Great Northern beans, in a pinch, and both David and Wolfert agree. My Balthazar recipe urges sticking to the beans of Tarbais, the native bean, from around Auch in the foothills of the Pyrenees. "Seek them out for their fat and creamy texture—they are the soul of this dish." The S-word tends to appear often in descriptions of cassoulet, and the food of southern France generally.

In the end, I must lack conviction, for I couldn't find any damned Tarbais. I could get them shipped from D'Artagnan, the mail-order house of Auch-based André Daguin, as I could the duck confit. (It was Daguin who understood, as recently as the 1970s, that a duck breast could be sliced out and served rare, like a steak, thus saving it from the fat-poached parcel of confit du canard.) D'Artagnan packages a "Cassoulet Dinner" for $94.50 that includes a package of Tarbais, but the recipe they provide calls for Great Northerns. I declined the offer.

For my made-to-order dish, I errantly cooked only one pound, half the Balthazar amount, because I misread the directions. Result? A soupier cassoulet than should be. Beans scattered like flotsam on the surface, versus a tide of beans buoying all else up.

The sausage

S chleisman's of Yale Avenue, no longer in operation, made as fine a cassoulet sausage as can be had this side of the Midi. It was a Portuguese style, spicy and coarse. I know the maker used topnotch ingredients because, one, he couldn't afford to stay in business, and, two, I once ate half of a raw Portuguese before realizing it and lived to tell this tale:

"Can I help you?" he asked.

"Yeah, let me have two of the Portuguese."

"Liked that, did ya?" He'd remembered me.

"Delicious. Ate it for lunch. That's a smoked sausage … right?"

"Yeah, 14 hours. But it's cold smoked. So, you gotta cook it."

That first Portuguese plagued me for about a week. The sickness never hit hard enough to hobble, but sufficiently enough to reveal the parasites at work: slight, sturdy swirls of nausea centered in the gut. I battled them with hits of strong coffee and, in the evening, gin.

Coxe's *Great Book of Sausages* defines a Toulouse sausage as 3-1 of lean pork to hard back fat, ground by hand with plenty of chopped, raw garlic. It being October, I took the sentimental route and opted for bratwurst. Johnsonville brand, specifically, though I was tempted to have Siegi, my other sausage monger, grind up something on the spot. (Siegi's sausages, while delicious, are too fine a grind for this dish.) For a pound or so, it hardly seemed worth the effort. And anyway, a strong, fatty Johnsonville fit the bill.

The fat

L ard was the plan. My local grocer, answering the call from an increasingly Spanish-speaking clientele, had begun selling it in handy butter-sized quarters for about a buck. On my shopping trip, the quarters were gone and, in their place, one-gallon pails. All I needed was half a cup for sweating the aromatics. Oddly, probably four times that amount was rendered out of the carnitas I would be tossing into the pot with the sausage. Such is the full-circled ritual of cassoulet, taking out fats and putting them back in.

The Balthazar recipe called for duck fat, which I could probably find at a foodie-infested counter I had in mind. But in the interest of going whole hog, I bought some salt pork.

The final step of a proper cassoulet is, in effect, a culmination of the penultimate. After the last meats are gently stirred into the stew, a layer of chopped parsley and fresh breadcrumbs is spread across the whole. The fats that would otherwise slick the surface are absorbed, forming a rich crust that crowns the bubbling lot. The aroma, by this time, is pure torture. Herald angels can be heard singing praises. Dinner is close.

The confit

B ack to Daguin's duck: Remaining after the bisection of breasts from the carcass are the leg and thigh. These are meaty, flavorful pieces that find their way onto more Languedoc menus than grilled-rare breast. Preserving them is something of a science. The quarters are poached in duck fat until they render most of their own fat and all of their blood. Then they are placed in jars and covered in the poaching fat to preserve. (Similar to a local root beer purveyor I know, who keeps his recipe by adding onto the original vat, the fat of one duck goes to make the confit of another.) To serve, the quarters are quickly crisped in a sauté pan or on the grill. The fat is all but depleted and the meat moist, succulent and memorable.

Again, duck being problematic, I stuck with pig. Conveniently enough, the barrios of east Tulsa sell fresh pork confit in the form of carnitas, which translates to "little meats." Different beast, same process: the pork chunks are slow-simmered in their own fat (lard) until cooked. I don't comprehend the science of confit, even if I admire the alchemy. And, as Child said, the meat flavors, after all is said and done, tend to blend into one another, making cassoulet perhaps the ultimate melting pot.

The pork

A young butcher in a posh part of town who promised to save me a belly from his next order of pork never phoned. That made five pigmen by the wayside. But I'd no time for an elegy.

My go-to grocer sells an "Arkansas bacon." It might be a bacon, but it tastes and chews and looks like a ham. Coupled with the lard, it would have made hog heaven. In lieu of lard, I sautéed the meat and vegetables in a cup of salt pork, the pink and white slab of stuff stored in the more challenging end of the butcher's case.

Coda: As it happened, I improvised more than usual, perhaps going overboard in my effort to localize a regional classic. My goal was to translate cassoulet, to bridge the gulch that separated the canned pork-and-beans of my snot-nosed youth with l'especialité du maison of our beloved if borrowed Languedoc. Well, ultimately I failed. But, same with trying to speak French, it kept me in the game. And of course, dinner was still served. I filled three bowls, poured three goblets of tannic syrah, and sent a good friend off on another of his world travels with a full belly. If only he could have figured out a way to haul it, there was enough cassoulet to get him there and back.

All of this experimentation and lamentation taught me a lesson: A cassoulet cooked in my kitchen may be called that out of convenience only. By promixity, it can never be my creation. In that respect, the name is meaningless, ambiguous and far-fetched. And so should it be.

A shop in San Francisco called Fog City News stocks its shelves with one-third newspapers, magazines and journals and two-thirds chocolate bars from the world over, for a robust 67 percent blend of cacao to other content. The good news of real chocolate is spreading, ironically at Fog City News, where the rest of the story seems ready to crawl into a cool, dark, snake-thick cave for a long winter's nap.

CHAPTER VII

THE MILKING OF CHOCOLATE

It seemed more a drink for pigs, than a drink for humanity.
Girolamo Benzoni, *History of the New World*, 1575

Up; and being ready, went by agreement to Mr. Blandsand
there drank my morning draught in good Chocolatte, and
slabbering my band sent home for another.
Samuel Pepys' Diary, 3 May 1664

O n day two of his first Seattle vacation, my young
son fell on the sidewalk in front of Theo Chocolate,
bloodying both knees and killing momentum.
After that, poor Lucas didn't want chocolate or anything else,
only to disappear. We hugged him, rubbed his shoulders, and
walked him down to Fremont Canal, the lane that transports
boat traffic between Shilshole Bay and Lake Union. He cried,
cursed his fate, and wouldn't look at the water. The free tour

of the factory that used to house Redhook Brewery didn't get any better. He and his brother balked at the obligatory hair nets, the noise was grating and the chocolate less comforting to a kid than a foiled kiss. My boy freaked at the fig-fennel, Earl Grey, and burnt-sugar confections. This foreignness in the name of chocolate all but collapsed him. We ended up rolling him out in the stroller, spending no time in the lobby of all-you-can-eat chocolate. All around the room were inviting plates of dark squares, what the French call *palet d'or*. But no Ghana or Madagascar for Lucas, no nib brittle, no "Bread and Dark Chocolate" squares, the buttered baguette crumbs crunching gently within Theo's lustrous dark concoction. The Fair Trade boast was lost on him, even the famed Fremont rocket, spent and strapped to a building up the street. How many neighborhoods claim a rocket, let alone a seven-ton statue of V.I. Lenin, a large troll sculpted into an underpass and, get this, two independent bookstores? How many 'hoods get to smell the chocolate as it melts, blends, and becomes the rich, black mystery that it is? And how many young boys and girls, I wondered, fell prey to the lure of infinite chocolate only to find a bitter end?

There are chocolate makers and then there are fondeurs. The makers take the cacao pods and process them for the fondeurs who take the raw product and melt it, flavor it, and mold it to make confection. In a good year, the world's 15 million acres of cacao will yield 3 million tons of beans—half that of the coffee crop. Ninety percent of it is grown by farmers with small plots, 12 acres or less. Africa accounts for 70 percent of all cacao, the Ivory Coast carrying the lion's share.

Many who work wonders with chocolate have never seen a cacao tree. Few who slave in the tropical settings perfect for cacao have eaten a bonbon. Cacao thrives 20 degrees either side of the equatorial belt, in moist, hot, and consequently third-world conditions. Where chocolate grows on trees.

Of chocolate grades, there are three: The *criollo* of Mesoamerica is more disease prone and produces fewer pods. It is prized if not prolific. The South American *forastero* accounts for 80 percent of the world's cacao crop. A hybrid of the two emerged in 18th-century Trinidad—the *trinitario*. *Nacional*, a fourth, grew in Ecuador before falling victim to witch's broom, a smothering outgrowth of fungus. In the late 1990s, on a plantation near Venezuela's Lake Maracaibo, 300 *criollo* trees were planted at Chuao, in hopes of rallying a comeback.

Cacao pods cling to tree trunks, below the leaves, anchored like Christmas ornaments. Ripe, they are the color of tie-dye. The pods are carefully cut from their roots and then cracked with a machete. If any bean is damaged by the blade, it risks spoiling the rest—the proverbial bad apple.

The beans and the pulpy mass that envelops them are put in a vessel—traditionally, in a canoe—to ferment. The pulp liquefies and drains from the beans, which by now have taken on flavor characteristics. They are then air dried in the sun and put into 130-pound jute bags for transport. The farmer's work is thus done.

At the factory, the processing begins with a roasting, then a winnowing to separate the husk from the nibs, the pure cacao. The nibs are milled to create cocoa liquor—pure, unrefined cacao with its butter. Until 1828, cooks separated cocoa from its butter by boiling and skimming. Then Coenraad van Houten invented a hydraulic press that would squeeze the butter from the chocolate, leaving what's called a presscake that could then be properly ground into powder. When van Houten added potassium or sodium carbonates to the powder, so that it would better blend with hot water, he created "Dutch process," which darkens the powder but blunts the flavor.

In good chocolate, a bit of the butter goes back in to create the velvety substance that inspires true chocolatiers. Most often, however, the butter goes off to Lancome and the like. Cost-saving vegetable fats are used in its place. Either way, cocoa and fat come together through conching, invented by Rudolphe Lindt, another Swiss, in 1879. Using heavy rollers to pound the nibs against a curved bed—Lindt's was shaped like a sea shell, hence conch—he squeezed the air from the chocolate to smooth out the graininess.

Tempering, a controlled cooling of heated chocolate for the purpose of stabilizing, completes the cycle.

L ike the bags of coffee beans stacked on the floor of a good roastery, chocolate beans bear the distinction of place. No more than a cup of Yirgacheffe tastes like a Guatemalan, chocolates from the Ivory Coast and Madagascar taste completely, even exotically, different. At least in their native states.

The way milk tilts a cappuccino toward the flavor universal, milk castrates the flavor of chocolate, cutting the nut from its living seed. Whatever chocolate was in its native state, milk plainly dilutes it. Like anything processed for profit, milk chocolate is an alteration of the original intent, a complex ballet of deliberate adulteration, market spin and consumer behavior. Removed so far from its source, chocolate in effect ceases to be.

A 1991 study by A.J. Hill and L. Heaton-Brown revealed that chocolate accounted for nearly half of all food cravings.[1] Valrhona, the French firm, employs a jury of 10 whose full-time job it is to taste-test new products. Craving and slaving, the world devours cacao however brown and milky sweet. The jury is out as to whether chocolate lovers are craving chocolate or sugar.

But the judgment of chocolate is at hand. Guardians, protectors, and guerillas operating in the name of pure chocolate are rising up. Paris has its Club des Croqueurs de Chocolat, London its Chocolate Society, whose mantra is: "These dietary villains [sugar, saturated vegetable fat, powdered milk] are responsible for chocolate's un-deserved reputation as a fattening, tooth-rotting, addictive indulgence."

---

1 The Marquis de Sade, the original eroticist, was mad for chocolate. "Chocolate inspired an irre-sistible passion," writes Maurice Lever, his biographer. During his long stays in jail, Sade's standing chocolate order to outside friends included ground chocolate and mocha coffee, chocolate biscuits and pastilles, crème au chocolat, myriad bars, and, for his piles, cacao butter suppositories.

The modern cosmetics industry pays a premium for cocoa butter, leaving many chocolate firms a cheap out. The European Union famously made it legal for producers to use up to five percent of cocoa butter substitute and the end product still be labeled chocolate. At this passing, chocolatier Christian Constant draped his Paris doorway in black. The cocoa butter equivalents (CBEs) are limited to these six oils: palm oil, karate, illipe, sal, kokum and mango-kernel. To be called *chocolat*, French law requires a minimum 32 percent cacao, which makes most of the world's chocolate mere candy.

The world eats about $42 billion of chocolate a year, the vast bulk of it milk chocolate. Per capita, Switzerland eats 22.7 pounds a year, though that figure includes tourists in Switzerland eating chocolate. Cocoa beans trade on the commodities market, crops purchased years in advance to stabilize the price in case of natural or political havoc.

In 2008, Campbell Soup Company sold its Godiva brand to Ülker of Istanbul. Former Godiva CEO Eugene Dunkin liked to emphasize the packaging and presentation of his product, aiming at the jugular of the American bonbon eater and listening for what he called "the glorious gasp." Godiva was founded on Brussels' Grand Place by Joseph Draps. At Campbell Soup, chocolate was about appearance first and flavor second. "Across America," Dunkin said, "we are the gold standard, equivalent to Tiffany's little blue box."

People have coveted chocolate from day one, starting with the Mixteca, the early tribes of Mexico.

In the Nahuatl currencies of 1545, 100 cacao beans would buy you a turkey hen, a jackrabbit, 100 large tomatoes, 33 newly picked avocados (or 100 ripe ones), or 100 tamales. Certain lecherous Aztecs would counterfeit pure cacao with such fillers as avocado pits, wax, amaranth dough, ashes, and chalky earth. In Nicaragua, where cacao beans were bartered on a system of 20, eight or 10 would buy a prostitute.

Colha, a Maya excavation site in northern Belize, has relinquished ceramics dating back to 600 B.C. A theobromine compound detected on their insides provides proof of chocolate.[2]

The lab at Hershey Foods Technical Center employs a process called liquid chromatography to mine the insides of archaeological finds, scraping for evidence of cacao. They estimate chocolate goes back 38 centuries, predating even the San Lorenzo Olmecs (1200–900 B.C.) of oldest Mexico.

It was the Swede Carolus Linnaeus, naturally, who classified chocolate Theobroma cacao ("elixir of the gods"), placing the Mesoamerican term second and his lord first, a classic European tradition of enlightened arrogance. It was the icing on the cake of Hernan Cortes, the Spaniard who crushed the Aztecs and stole their holy sweet.

Cacao grows on trees, in pods of 20 to 60 beans. Cocoa is what we make of those seeds—the industrialized aftermath that ships globally in bar, liquid, and powder form. Both words emanate from *kakawa*, a term native to the Isthmus of Tehuantepec, the wrist that foreshadows the fist of Yucatan in southernmost Mexico. The seeds were sewn and the legend grown.

The Toltecs, lords of Mesoamerica prior to the Aztecs, worshipped Quetzalcoatl, who bestowed upon them cacao from the garden of Paradise. Ultimately, Quetzalcoatl (the Plumed Serpent) got crossways with Tezcatlipoca (the Smoking Mirror) and fled east on a raft of woven snakes. Vipers must have been everywhere in the ancient city. As prophesied, Quetzalcoatl returned to Tenochtitlan triumphant, but so did Cortes at about the same time. The Aztec good life was undone.[3]

The story of cacao is one of peasants and priests, snakes and sacrifice. Cacao thrives beneath rainforest growth and suffers when such canopy is slashed and burned. Rats gnaw at its pods

---

2 A drawing in the Madrid Codex—an ancient book written on tree bark—depicts four Maya gods piercing their own ears with obsidian lancets. Their blood waters cacao pods strewn at their feet. Maya elite were laid to rest robed in jaguar pelts and jade bracelets. Next to their beds were placed bowls of chocolate to sustain them on their journey. The Opossum God, when he hit the sacred road carrying the Rain God on his back, fueled his zeal with hits of hot chocolate. The Maya seemed always to be going someplace.

3 Though the Aztecs preferred a cool drink, Maya chocolate was hot. Explained Laura Esquivel, who named her book, *Like Water for Chocolate*: "It's a very old expression. I think from colonial times, for when someone is so angry that they are about to boil over but are still contained."

from the ground and monkeys yank them from above. Serpents[4] of ill repute—green mambas, black mambas, Gaboon vipers, and mapepire z'ananna, the bushmaster, a snake half the distance of a first down—run thick where cacao thrives.

The Yucatan peninsula and its adjacent plains were chocolate hotbeds, places like Chontalpa in Tabasco, coastal Chiapas, Boca Costa in the volcanic piedmont, Xoconochco, and Tula, in the Guatemalan highlands. A painting in the Temple of the Owls of Chichen Itza portrays a serpent curled, open-mouthed, beneath a ceiling of hanging cacao pods. The Yucatan was legendary for its sinkholes of cacao, swollen spots of wet earth capable of managing the tree growth that the relatively dry highlands could not.

In a mysterious ritual, Maya youth were baptized in a mixture of flowers, water culled from tree trunks and stone pools, and pounded cacao, dabbed on the forehead with a dipped bone. Mysterious because who, if anybody, brought the task of baptism to the pagan Maya? Pagan or not, they were not without ritual. Chokola'j meant to "drink chocolate together." Newly wedded Chol Maya of Chiapas exchanged five grains of cacao, among other coveted things.

The chocolate of old was not eaten but drunk, frothed by repeatedly pouring the mixture head high from a vessel into a bowl on the ground. The Lacandon Maya of east Chiapas drank a drink of cacao, water, sugar cane and toasted corn. The chocolate was ground on a heated stone called a metate, and frothed with a wooden swizzle stick called a molinillo—a latterday M&M, as it were. Later Maya recipes included chiles, vanilla, and honey, with achiote seeds to color it red. (French children still drink Banania, a powdered drink of cocoa, banana flour, cereals, honey and sugar. Its logo depicts a Senegalese in a tassled fez. The recipe was inspired by a native drink of La Managua, Nicaragua.

A Franciscan missionary named Bernardino de Sahagun wrote a description of a Tenochtitlan peddler of tlaquetzalli, or "precious thing":

---

4 "You know tonka beans?" asks Trinidadian Chuck Ramkissoon—the Jay Gatsby of Flatbush Avenue—of his friend Hans in Joseph O'Neill's *Netherland*. "The seed was used for perfume, snuff. Nowadays, they've got synthetic products, so the old plantations are returning to forest. Same thing with cocoa. That business stopped because of the snakes. People were no longer prepared to gamble with death."

She grinds cacao [beans]; she crushes, breaks, pulverizes them. She chooses, selects, separates them. She drenches, soaks, steeps them. She adds water sparingly, conservatively; aerates it, filters it, strains it, pours it back and forth, aerates it; she makes it form a head, makes foam; she removes the head, makes it thicken, makes it dry, pours water in, stirs water into it.

A 17th-century Londoner, Dr. Henry Stubbes, advocated chocolate for any number of sexual maladies, not least for "Supplying the Testicles with a Balsam." Francois Pralus, a chocolatier of Roanne, France, paints abstracts of women, smearing his canvases with a chocolate-dipped brush. He makes a pure Chuao chocolate that he describes in one word: leather. A Kiev chocolatier, Andrei Korkunov, crafts a finger-shaped bonbon of dark chocolate cloaking pork fat. Chocolate incites crazy passions.

For 40 days, the finest Aztec slave was forced to impersonate the great Quetzalcoatl in a death dance that had him raving through the day, gorging on chocolate, and jailed at night. When the slave grew resigned to his sacrificial fate, he was made to swallow a drink called itzpacalatl, or "water from the washing of obsidian blades," otherwise known as a gourd of chocolate tainted with the blood of sacrifice. Then his heart was extracted before his eyes with said obsidian blade, which sounds both more painful and poetic than a Bowie knife.

Women were banished from St. Cristobal de la Casas for drinking chocolate during high mass. They got back at the hypocritical priest by poisoning his chocolate. In Mexico, before they ripped out all the criollo, chocolate was God.[5]

Chloë Doutre-Roussel's chocolate consumption could slay a priest in a cloister. Chloë, 99-pound author of *The Chocolate*

5 *Zen Wrapped in Karma Dipped in Chocolate: A Trip Through Death, Sex, Divorce, and Spiritual Celebrity in Search of the True Dharma* by Brad Warner came out in 2010. I missed it. *Simply Relevant Chocolate Boutique: Relational Bible Series for Women*, by Group Publishing (2007), seems like dirty pool, chocolate being a tease more than even a subtext. Off of Amazon: "This is the participant guide for a relational, interactive and learner based study on Grace. Each session involves some kind of food ... for week 1 think Cracker Jacks and chocolate truffles!! Week 1 focuses on the story of the Prodigal Son. ... Get ready to experience God's grace with the women in your church!"

Connoisseur,[6] eats a pound-plus of chocolate a day. She eats and adds to a chocolate "database" of beans, percentages, producers, fondeurs, and flavor profiles, and has since age 14. She calls her work evangelism, "spreading the word" about the goodness of good chocolate. "I pride myself on my ability to 'bring the choco-light' to anyone willing to discover and enjoy the finest chocolate."

Chloë keeps chocolate in her closets and under her bed. She is not hiding them. Chocolate cannot hide from Chloë. Her bedroom, her boudoir du chocolat, stays an edgy 59 degrees Fahrenheit to keep the chocolate safe. She once bought chocolate for Fortnum & Mason, the London department store, beating out 2,999 chocoholics who applied for the job. Chloë's resume did not have to proclaim, "Because I love chocolate!" She doesn't eat chocolate for breakfast, she eats it before, when her palate is at its freshest.

Chloë believes that most chocoholics are milk chocolate sugar addicts, easily won and wary of the dark side. She coaches novices to work out a chocolate "profile" for the purposes of determining passion. "If, on the other hand, you are like me, and chocolate is the main focus of your life, you may find you need to reassess your priorities to give it the space it needs." Chloë writes sentences like that without blushing. "If you are like me and like to eat three different types of filled chocolates every day ..." In a chapter titled, "Chocolate: Friend or Foe?" she begins by inquiring of your "emotional relationship" to chocolate.

She eats chocolate between meals, not because she's hungry but because that's when her taste buds are the most in need of a fix. "You should be able to derive a more intense pleasure from the chocolate," she argues, "making it also easier not to overeat." She sleeps less than six hours a night. She swims an hour a day and has for 20 years. Even when she's not eating chocolate, she's eating chocolate. Her body burns through it like a furnace blasting carbon.

---

6 Books on chocolate abound. Anymore, they lack the sanctity of the Maya texts, if not the lust. A few titles I found scanning Amazon: *Chocolate Epiphany, Chocolate Obsession, Naked Chocolate, Indulgence, Absolutely Chocolate, Pure Chocolate, Better Than Sex, Death by Chocolate*—part of a series—*The Chocolate Cake Sutra, Enlightened Chocolate, Chocolate: A Healthy Passion.* Many of the covers feature brown to near-black molten chocolate dripping onto something flaky and baked. An entire erotica subset exists, the cover usually depicting a blonde bowing at the altar of a muscular black man. My favorite: *Oysters & Chocolate: Erotic Stories of Every Flavor* by Jordan LaRousse and Samantha Sade.

Chloë counters the portent of bad news with half a bar of chocolate. Don't eat chocolate when you feel depressed. Eat it in anticipation of depression, says Chloë, and you'll probably eat less. When she bought for Fortnum & Mason, her life revolved around chocolate. Like it did before the job, like it does now. Like it will until we cover her grave in cocoa powder and smear chocolate liquor onto her headstone.

The English taste for milky treats ultimately drove Chloë from her post. The pound she consumed on her own plus the Fortnum & Mason pound she tasted and spit in the same day, she likened to "selling your body by day and having a boyfriend at night." Chloë divines men as she makes her way through her chocolate day. In one of the Italian brand Amedei's burnt caramel, she once conjured "a young, beautiful man, full of fire, the kind that Pier Paolo Pasolini liked in his films."

Chocolate entered Europe in the hold of a Portuguese caravel, from Veracruz, in 1585. In the early 17th century, Jewish artisans, kicked around in Spain and Portugal, settled into the nook of Bayonne in Basque country, where they became France's first chocolatiers. The Pyrenees protected them and sequestered their chocolates. Over the Med to the boot, a Florentine merchant named Carletti was pumping chocolate into Italy. Chocolate's long and winding road—from early, New World expertise to Old World exploration—seems to be finally connecting.

On its Web site, Seattle's Theo Chocolate says that it "is Proud to be the only Organic, Fair Trade, Bean-To-Bar Chocolate Factory in the United States." Our tour guide threw the Fair Trade line out pretty heavily, in a way typically reserved for coffee retailers. She made hard sells for Theo's Origin Bars: Costa Rica 91 percent, Ghana 84, Ghana-Panama-Ecuador 75, Ivory Coast 75, Madagascar 74. At Theo and elsewhere, chocolate has become a game of percentages.

Denver chocolatier Steve De Vries has a motto: "One hundred years behind the times." That's his way of saying he wants to make chocolate more like a Maya and less like a Mars. He counts Chloë, Countess Chocolat, among his fans.

The only flavor I consistently get out of a glass of wine is cherry, enlarged by the collision of the wine with protein, say a bloody steak or a crusty chicken. It is usually courtesy of a grape from the family of vines that thrive in the Languedoc of our not-so-recent-anymore sabbatical. Grenache is the most dominant of these, along with syrah. Carignan, mourvedre, and cinsault round out the house. The easiest way to tell them apart is to drink them singly, in 100-percent bottlings, versus blends. By themselves, each tastes specific, singular and purposeful. It takes years of practice, though, to tell them apart, and even a year of bottles was not enough for me.

CHAPTER VIII

VINTAGE SMITH

The Lost Weekenders were seated on the lawn, awaiting instruction, when their leader emerged from the house holding aloft a portrait of Bob Wills.

"He comes stumbling out with the Sara Bowersock painting," said Scott Large. "For the rest of the two days, Bob went with us everywhere. He was the official mascot—on the bus, in the vineyard, the bar, wherever we went that night.

"The spirit of Bob."

To appreciate how winemaker Charles Smith, his Oklahoma rep Scott Large, Tulsa artist Sara Bowersock, and Texas Playboy Bob Wills go together, you have to understand a little bit about blending. And Lost Weekends.

Smith, Washington winemaker du jour—one of the hottest things in wine since the 1976 Judgment of Paris, when the French got their asses handed to them by the Californians—is the force behind K Vintners, whose "Kung Fu Girl" has been making wine drinkers out of beer drinkers and Riesling fans out of most. To reward the biggest promoters of "Kung Fu Girl," Smith threw a three-day hoedown of food, wine, and controlled mayhem: the Lost Weekend. Oklahoma drank enough of it to earn both Large and Alex Kroblin, his Thirst Merchants partner, spots on the list.

"He started out at 2,000 cases and now he's at 75,000 cases a year, all of it from the same vineyard, all hand-picked," said Large, whose Thirst Merchants owes 10 percent of its portfolio to Smith. "And he makes 'Kung Fu Girl' the same way he makes his 'Royal City' Syrah. You just don't find that."

More miraculous, perhaps, is that Smith found us. Tulsa was not on Smith's radar when Large called and said K wines needed to be in Oklahoma, nor was it when he came to town in the autumn of '09 for a Thirst portfolio tasting and wine dinner hosted by Lucky's on Cherry Street. But Smith has a way of taking over a city's airspace. So after a quick "breakfast, lunch, and dinner" that featured farm eggs, pancakes, lamb sausage—with the 2007 K Viognier, served in a coffee cup—chicken-fried bacon BLT, tuna casserole, cold pizza (in individual "used" pizza boxes), and cold fried quail with sage gravy, Smith and Company went out.

"At some point in the night," Large recalled, "when we were all at the wine bar (Vintage 1740), Charles decided he wanted to pretend he got hit by a car. We'd been going back and forth across the street from 1740 to the Mercury Lounge, getting pretty crazy. So he said, 'I'm going to lay in the street and you guys pull your car up like you just hit me and let's do a photo shoot.' So now there are all these 'dead' photos of Charles at 18th and Boston."

Before he left town, Smith loaded up on T-shirts at Dwelling Spaces; ate back to back to back at Coney Island, Weber's, and Nelson's Ranch House; proposed to the love of his life, a drop-dead Roman named Ginevra Casa, at the Full Moon Café where he, in his words, "proceeded to drink my face off"; and spent some $10,000 at Parkhill on South Lewis. Restocking his cellar from the Lost Weekend.

The idea was to reward 34 wine reps across the country who'd kicked butt in a 2010 "Kung Fu Girl" sales contest. A tireless promoter, Smith uses such opportunities to show appreciation and just plain show off. For their efforts—and their pains—Smith awarded the lucky 34 with a trip to Walla Walla, a multi-course Italian feast on his front lawn, and bag of ibuprofen, water, and phone numbers to the local police and emergency medical units.

"He hit this one guy so hard in the face with his fist," said Large. "Kind of slapped him a little bit. It was wild."

A wine drinker of utmost sincerity, Smith keeps about 2,000 bottles on hand, for personal use. In a game called "Raid the Cellar," a runner from each of five tables ran to the cellar to pick any bottle in Smith's collection. Two rules: One, there had to be at least one other bottle of whatever you grabbed still on the shelf. Two, no sharing with other tables, not even a smell. Breaking either rule would result in immediate elimination and no more wine.

Which, to Smith, must border on hell's own kitchen. Large and the other Lost Weekenders drank, between them, 32 bottles, everything from 30-year-old Dom Perignon to great Burgundies and Bordeaux. Generosity is part of Smith's charm, but the message being served in every glass was one of respect and acknowledgment, of being on the same page.

"The idea is that we didn't serve *my* wine with lunch. It wouldn't be pearls before swine. That's no fun, right? The trip was very little about my wine. It was more like this is what I do, and this is how I throw a party."

So right. Nor would it be a Charles Smith show without a road trip. The Lost Weekend began with a party at Smith's Anchor Bar in nearby Waitsburg, with DJ Howie Piro Intoxica! (the bass player in Danzig, for a stint) spinning records and The Big John Bates Grindshow providing rockabilly and burlesque. Not all of Waitsburg's 1250 citizens appreciated the invitation, though all were invited.

"I was born and raised in Holland, so nothing shocks me," said Imbert Mathee, the owner the *Waitsburg Times*, who covered the event. "They were more dressed than me when I go to the beach."

"I sold 200 tickets to the public," Smith said, in effort to make everybody feel welcome. "So, basically, I created a party around them. It was simply, 'You guys won, you're supposed to be having fun.' Not like some insurance seminar. They got the anti-pitch."

Best part about the Lost Weekend is how close *we* were to hosting it. Explaining his concept, aware of how nutty it sounded, Smith cracked a smile.

"Initially, we were thinking about bringing everybody to Tulsa. We really considered taking it on the road somewhere."

You can see the elements coming together ... concert at the Cain's, coneys and corndogs to soak up the wine, a truck from Parkhill or Ranch Acres, or both, pulled up to the ballroom alongside an EMSA truck, red lights spinning, and a tour bus ready to haul everybody back to the hotel so that the rep from Hawaii who threw up on the guy from Washington wouldn't end up on, say, Boston Avenue with his pleats around his knees and Tulsa's finest ready to add cuffs.

Is this any way to run a winery? It is if you're Charles Smith, *Food & Wine* Winemaker of the Year, the antichrist of the wine trade, its John the Baptist, at least, waist-deep in a steady stream, drinking mead and tearing the wings off locusts, finding converts around every bend.

"Two different Winemaker of the Year awards, 300 points in a row from Robert Parker for 'Royal City.' It's not in terms of volume," said Large, "it's the wake he leaves. The wave he's causing."

"He's very different from traditional winemakers. Not his wines, but the way he markets them," said Philippe Garmy, organizer of the OSU Wine Forum. "It's like heavy-metal counterculture. Each of his syrahs is one of Ozzy Osbourne's children."

"The guy's been a big success, and everybody's realized that, even though he doesn't do it the traditional way," said Duane Wollmuth of the very much a mouthful Walla Walla Wine Valley Association. "He's gained a lot of respect because he has been out there doing it his own way. Charles is definitely making some quality wines. It's certainly not a 'Two-Buck Chuck' type of thing."

Out there meaning the Smith place in Mill Creek Road, the antebellum home of K Vintners, where the ankle-deep Titus Creek cuts a clear if tiny swath between an award-winning vineyard of stone and bone and the bluegrass lawn that laps at the wraparound porch. Out there, meaning, out there.

Why Walla Walla? Why not!

"I didn't move to Walla Walla because this is where the action was," Smith said. "It still isn't here! It was not my intention to get great reviews. I didn't run to get the wreath. I ran to run. The wine business is a gauntlet. If you stop, you die."

Smith isn't even the largest winemaker in Walla Walla, let alone Washington. Walla Walla's Precept Wines owns several brands, among them the Magnificent ·Wine Co., Smith's first winery, the one where he launched his now-legendary House label (House Wine, Steak House, Fish House). But with his Modernist Project—a series that includes the can't-miss labels "Velvet Devil" Merlot, "Boom Boom!" Syrah, and, his calling card, "Kung Fu Girl" Riesling, Smith is making new history.

Smith read the study that said 95 percent of all wine is drunk the day it's bought. The Modernist wines are meant to be drunk now and are priced for a market that doesn't cellar wine anyway. They all retail between $12 and $15 and all come with screwcaps instead of corks, which isn't unusual anymore but still sends a message.

"I'm not trying to trick them," Smith said of his fans and potential market. "I want them to be able to find the good bottle among the 30 for sale with the labels that say something fake, like something 'River' or something 'Lake' or 'Sky.' Mine bucks the trend by not trying to sell it as something you shouldn't have access to, like you're not a member of that club. I want to communicate the language of wine to everybody because not everybody speaks wine. If you use the language that people already have, they'll have easier access to your wine. You're doing them a favor and yourself a favor.

"Wine is for everybody. It's been for everybody forever. It's like bread. It's like tortillas or pasta."

It's partly this realization—that America is about to embrace what Europe has known for centuries—and partly Smith's ability as a winemaker that makes Garmy, among others, fans of the project.

"He embraces a spirit—a paradigm of the pioneer in winemaking. He's very democratic. He has a wine for everybody."

Even the entry-level wines defy industry standard. Other Thirst Merchant lines, like Owen Roe ("Sinister Hand") and Orrin Swift

("The Prisoner"), have caught on with consumers in the market for cool. But their entry level is a bit steeper than Smith's, and they lack his range. "You can either guzzle them, or read them," said Parkhill's Milton Leiter. "You can gloss over, or spend an entire evening. His go either way." Parkhill carries the Modernist line, but not the high-end Smith syrahs—big-sticker bottles better suited to a restaurant menu than a shop rack. "Syrah's a sticky wicket," Leiter said. "Especially $100 syrah. People know cabernet. They know what they're supposed to do with cab."

Leiter fields more requests for the easy-drinking Middle Sister "Forever Cool" Merlot or "Surfer Chick" Sauvignon Blanc than any of his beloved Costieres des Nimes. It's still retail, and that's consumer behavior. And if a wine shop is like a library—lots of titles gathering dust because nobody cracks them—then "some wines are Janet Evanovich and some are Ian McEwan." Meaning some wines are page-turners, while others give pause. What consumer picks which—the sexy thriller or the think piece—depends on that most elusive of labels: taste.

Smith's runs the gamut, and his policy of inclusion allows for monster bottles like the rich, red beast he calls "The Hustler," a syrah so transformed that its aroma of roast pork and flavor of black licorice (Smith doesn't do red) makes it an enticement, if not a steal, at $140. The *Wine Advocate* speculates the 2003 "Hustler" will peak in 2035. By then, the Middle Sister should be well into menopause.

"I like him, he knows what's he's doing," Leiter said. "And if there's growth to be had in the market, it should be there, in that $10–$15 range."

In America, wine tends to flow east, over the divide and into the middle trough. The bulk of it comes from Napa and Sonoma, but also Oregon's Willamette Valley and Washington's Columbia River Valley. It's there, or in the runoff of there, that Smith set up shop.

Walla Walla used to be known for its sweet strawberries and sweeter onions, Walla Walla Sweets, a bulb so fine they named a minor league ball club after it. Since the arrival of Smith—you might say his rise has coincided with that of the region—wine's taken over. Washington wine was on the rise, but Walla Walla remained an unknown quantity. Sweetness aside, you can't build a tourist trade on the strength of an onion. Then Smith bought an antebellum farmhouse on Mill Creek Road and there went the neighborhood. That he slept on the floor his first year and subsisted on Top Ramen and taco wagon is less sexy than his antics, or even his hair.

"I can't say I've always done the right thing. Maybe I drink too much and say the wrong words in front of the wrong people sometimes, but the idea is at least I'm authentic. People look at me like I must be cheating. A lot of people love my wine, and that's awesome. But, as with any business, if you stick your neck out, you're going to get a few lumps and bruises. But, if you stay in your shell, you'll get nothing."

W alla Walla is that weirdest of places, so familiar, so not. You've heard of it, imagine you can ... imagine it, only to find that it's hiding in a middle of nowhere more stuck than your own. And if you're coming from Seattle, it's even stucker.

Washington has two uneven sides, green and blonde, the Seattle side and the Other side. The coasts get the traffic and the press, but it's the rest with its Columbia River Valley and wheat fields that run to Canada that's throwing up dust in the world of wine. To get there from Seattle, you cross the Yakima River Valley, where the Rattlesnake Hills rise and the Cascades fade into a lush memory. Further on, toward the confluence of the Columbia and Snake rivers, the land flattens and the hills become round, routine, and endless. There is a suggestion of Big Sky country as the Blue Mountains lay a backdrop over the Tri-Cities area, where the roads and rivers bend.

Walla Walla is a Nez Perce term meaning "place of many waters." And some of the waters turn to wine.

Thirteen miles west of Walla Walla sits little Lowden, home to L'Ecole No. 41 and Woodward Canyon, two respected wineries in the region. Ten years ago, the local wine industry consisted of 30 wineries and 800 acres of vineyards, according to an association timeline. Now it's more than 100 wineries and nearly 2000 acres.

On a billboard there, the new poster child of Washington wine lurks behind a pair of shades and more hair than all of Winger combined. Welcome, says Charles Smith, a California escapee who rides the golden hills around Walla Walla on his 1947 Harley-Davidson Knucklehead, hair pulled back in a five-pound knot (unleashed, it swells and falls like the Gardens of Babylon), the summer sun raspberrying his Ray-Banned face—the pariah and pretty boy who puts his money where his oversized mouth is.

"You gotta spend some to get some," Smith says of his $8400 roadside attraction. "Eventually they'll come here. Maybe."

Here is a place far removed, especially for a guy like Smith, who left his west Seattle wine shop to come make wine, and before that left Copenhagen, where he'd followed his Danish girlfriend, where he hung out in night clubs managing rock bands, where everybody had really long hair, wore rock 'n' roll clothes and was good-looking, Smith claims, "because they're Danish."

"I moved here to do what I do, and I didn't know it would turn out like it did. Come on ... Copenhagen, Denmark, to Walla Walla, Washington? I moved here because this is not for the faint of heart."

Smith set up shop in Walla Walla ten years ago, but his evolution in wine goes back to his youth, when he slaved in restaurant kitchens as a 19-year-old. As a busboy at the Palm Springs Hilton, he dumped a tray of orange juice into the lap of Roger Smith, then-chairman of General Motors (and soon-to-be subject of filmmaker Michael Moore's *Roger & Me*).

"The head chef chased me out of the kitchen with a large knife," said Smith, who turned 50 in August. "But he weighed 300 pounds and I was a skinny, poor 140, and I ran backward giving him the finger. Until I fell, then I got up and ran really fast."

When he stopped running, he came to his senses.

"You work in a kitchen you work the longest hours, doing the dirtiest work to get paid the least. That sucks. I realized that the guy who had the best job was the guy who bought the wine. He gets to come in later, leave earlier, and he gets to drink all night. I'm like, 'That's my kind of job!' I excelled at that."

A Sacramento native whose dad sold used cars until he starting cutting hair under the sobriquet "Mr. Andre," Smith embraced his calling and honed his chops. He lined his mouth with the yeast and must of untold vintages, starting in his own backyard.

"I learned in Napa Valley," he said. "And I don't mean sitting in the tasting room listening to Windham Hill. I'd be in the cellar, the music's cranked, and you're drinking wine from a barrel. That's where it's going on."

Smith got his first glimpse of Washington not in a winery but from the front seat of a Chevy Astro van. He and one of his charges—Sune Rose Wagner, lead singer of The Raveonettes, a Danish indie rock duo—were on a three-month road trip doing what rockers do best.

"That's how I found it. I wasn't looking for it. I didn't even know I was going to make wine. I had $5000. I could hardly make anything."

A high-plains drifter of sorts, Smith came to Walla Walla not to blend in but to stand out. Walla Walla is known for its cabernet and merlot, but Smith wanted to be known for something else. He made his name with K Syrah, a cheeky play on words but more a brand, like the kind you iron into a screaming calf. A head-high, white "K" greets you at the winery entrance on Mill Creek Road east of town.

"I was tired of the stupid Euro stories behind American wineries. Some faux chateau thing. I live in America and I wanted my winery to sound like it. You don't even have to be able to fuckin' say it and you'll be able to buy it in a wine shop. It's got a fuckin' K on it!"

When I met him, in his spanking-new tasting room that used to be a garage, the fire-red Bob Wills T-shirt wrapped around his trunk seemed to have shrunk a size. "I was home 23 days between January 12 and June 21," he said, "and weigh 23 pounds more."

Smith does nothing like you'd expect a winemaker to do it. He drives a car in the Walla Walla Fair demolition derby—a big, black sedan called the Battle Wagon, whose roof has a white skull with a black sword thrust through it. He calls it his day in the dunk tank. Hanging from the steel-and-wood rafters of his tasting room are four 90-pound woofers, for rocking the hard way when a dinner party or wine event calls for it. Cases of wine sit on pallets next to minimalist furniture. Light pours in like golden chardonnay. A menu of the available vintages is cut-and-pasted on a large wall in that graphically compelling, black-and-white K Vintners way. A six-glass "maximus" runs you $5.

"They'll get loud," Smith says not of the wines but the woofers, "but in a way that just sort of envelops you. It's a real, even sound."

To prove it, he cranks them and the air in the room begins to hum slightly. Your ears don't shrink but your chest swells. An older couple doing a tasting begins to swing dance. Napa seems a world away.

A few nights earlier, he'd thrown out the opening pitch for the Sweets, Walla Walla's representative in the West Coast League, where they play the likes of the Bend Elks, Bellingham Bells and Wenatchee Applesox. He'd been using his spacious tasting room as a bullpen.

"I actually have a great knuckleball," he said. "When I was 14, I was a pitcher. My knuckleball floats and then drops ... kaboom! Then I get to the park and they hand me an onion." So he threw a fastball. "A strike."

Not all of Smith's pitches find the plate. A few years back, he bought the Pastime, an Italian mom-and-pop that had been serving Walla Walla for 100 years. The move did not sit well with some of the locals, who view every move Smith makes with suspicion.

"He told me he's known around town as the guy who killed a pastime," said record-store owner Jim McGuinn. "But the guy was going to sell it to somebody."

McGuinn runs Hot Poop, one of those now-lost record shops that reek of incense and independence, where fans roam the stacks in silence beneath Beatles and Clash posters, concert fliers and a garage-like assortment of rock 'n' roll bric-a-brac. McGuinn, whose long hair has grayed from the rock of ages, was the town mystery man, before Smith came to town.

"I compare him to Levi Strauss," he said, meaning Smith left the safety of the city for the gold in the hills. "There are rumors—he gets his money from dealing heroin, he's a rich boy whose parents set him up. None of which is the truth.

"I like him. He took the edge off me being an eccentric."

"I got here at the right time," said Smith. "The economy was bad. People weren't buying plane tickets but they were still buying wine. The ones who were buying $40 bottles started buy $20, and the ones buying $20 were buying $10."

"People do the same thing with speakers," said McGuinn, who sold Smith a piece-meal stereo system when he hit town. He credits Smith's success to the mystique he removes from the traditionally reverent wine trade. "The only brands I usually buy are Annie Green Springs and Red Mountain. But my wife and I were in Bayside, Maine, one Fourth of July and we pulled into a little roadside shop for provisions. They had fireworks, watermelons, and both the 'House Red' and 'Kung Fu Girl' Riesling. I thought, 'Wow.' "

For all the notoriety, K Vintners comes not from a plan but an impulse. When he first got to Washington, Smith fell in with another transplant, Cayuse Vineyards' Christophe Baron, the first Frenchman to establish a wine estate in Washington. Baron begged him to come to Walla Walla, and sweetened the pot with enough fruit for 15 barrels of wine.

"He said I'll give you the grapes and you can pay me when you sell the wine," Smith said. "He was from France and he wanted somebody else who was no-bullshitting, tough, Euro-centric, knew about food and travel. He was my partner in crime."

"They each had capes made," said Large, "and they would walk around Walla Walla in these capes and I guess that's when people around there started to hate Charles. Nobody can keep up with him."

Or them. Baron and Smith were the "Toxic Twins," known for entering a restaurant with seven bottles of wine between them. "They'd say, how come you guys bring so much wine? We'd say, 'In case one of them's corked.' We'd drink six bottles of wine at dinner. We were the passionate ones."

Thus emboldened, Smith walked into a Seattle bank in June 2001 to ask for a line of credit. He'd been making wine for two years. He flipped through his business plan—an underwhelming three-pager with a spreadsheet and a couple of flowcharts—and explained away his odd job history. He spoke Washington wine with enough authority to get a sit down.

"They said we really like your idea and the people you're working with all look really good. I said, 'But I have no collateral.' They said, 'We'd like to taste your wine.' "

They all met, Smith and some bankers, at a wine bar the following day, he with a range of anonymous bottles—he had no bond and, hence, no winery name; he had no license and therefore no label.

"I filled their glasses, and they swirled it around, smelled it, tasted it, then the guy reaches out his hand and says, 'You got a deal. We're going to give you $250,000 and this wine is your collateral.' I'm like ... 'Awesome.' "

With the line of credit, he was able to find a property, create a label, buy a house. The latter dates to 1860. Coyotes roam near enough to keep the Shih Tzus under wraps. Behind it is the building that houses K Vintners. There's a temperature-controlled warehouse lined with barrels, and a tasting room he used before opening the one downtown. On the back of the house, down a rickety flight of steps, is his personal stash. It holds a couple of thousand bottles. Smith grabbed a French one and led the way.

Upstairs in the living room, a stray cat padded across the floorboards. The master sat back against a sofa, sipping at his glass, oblivious to the toy dog licking on his bare feet. Feet that soon will crush 120 tons of grapes—7000 cases worth. He'll climb into the 5-foot deep crusher and pound 4 feet of fruit into submission. He's looking forward to the exercise. "I can't wear most of my shirts and pants," he said, resting the glass of Chateauneuf du Pape on his belly. "A Domaine du Caillou. Pretty good, huh?"

Of course. It was good enough for popes. But I wanted to sample some of the house wine. He went to the cellar and brought up a pair of bottles: a 2005 vintage of "The Deal," from a place called the Wahluke Slope, and a 2007 version of "The Hustler." After the Chateauneuf, they were a mouthful. Like a dose of Jack Kerouac after a diet of Victor Hugo.

Smith, I learned from several videos online, would rather drink than talk, masticate than pontificate. Wine notes are a slippery slope, and he can talk tannins and balance and structure with the best of them. But he's better at just talking.

Smith does a wine called "Old Bones," a syrah that the *Wine Advocate's* Robert Parker gave 99 points and deemed "hedonistic." Its label (black-and-white, always) depicts a sword fight to the death, pitting against each other two crowned skeletons who can't and won't be killed. The story behind it goes:

When the house on Mill Creek Road was homesteaded in the mid-19th century, there was a log cabin there. In it lived a Native American who led a band of Indians out of the Blue Mountains. His name was Old Bones, and he befriended the man who owned Smith's house. Together, they would make trips to trade with the Indians of the Columbia River.

A small vineyard now sits between the house and the big K that marks the entrance. Smith was going to name the vineyard "Old Bones" in honor of those who'd come before him. But in the year the first vintage was ready for release, his neighbor died. He was an Indian named Phil Lane. And now, he has a vineyard named after him, with a clear-running, half-foot deep stream that separates it from the bluegrass lawn that surrounds Chateau Smith.

Tulsa and Walla Walla share two things, anyway—both sound more Indian than they now are, and both are seeking to be known for something by somebody from somewhere else. Smith found a sweet spot on the nowhere side of Washington to make his wine, an "oasis in a sea of wheat," a fellow transplant called it. But the middle of nowhere is a state of mind. Who knew that, when the wine revolution came, it would be led by a pig-tailed warrior girl pitching a sleepy German varietal? Who knew America, and Tulsa in it, was ready to take Riesling and like it?

"I was told it was going to be my kind of place," Smith said of our town. "I didn't go there because I was selling a huge amount of wine there. They liked what I was doing and embracing it and I wanted to come. Size-wise, for what I do, Oklahoma is an over-performer for its category.

"It's like me—I'm an over-performer for my category."

Smith could have stayed in Seattle, could have stayed away from Tulsa, could be 23 pounds lighter and however many pence none-the-richer. That's just not how he sets the scale.

"I had to give up a lot to come here, and I didn't give up that to get the jackpot. I got sleeping on the floor making 15 barrels of wine. What I have now is something different because of what I put into it, luck and timing and everything else.

"This is kind of the frontier, for people willing to risk it all."

We're in his Suburban, driving north, through so much waving wheat that I begin to get sea sick. The landscape has lost its scope. We could be anywhere, and nowhere.

"There's a camel," he says, interrupting a conversation on his cell. Another time he points out a pioneer cemetery, its crosses glowing bone white in the western sun. "I tried to buy that," Smith said, pointing to a cinema. "I wanted to do Sunday matinees, you know, for kids? Because there's nothing to do here."

Here is nowhere fast. Waitsburg, a little 'burg on the eastern edge of Washington, so far below Spokane that even Idaho is closer. Here is where the Smith ethic of pick yourself up by your bootstraps takes on significant meaning.

"I got $460,000 in the town," he tallies. "It gives this place value—value to me. You have to contribute to the community, to invest in it somehow."

One way would be to buy the defunct American Legion Post No. 35 and paint a big, black-and-white Stars and Stripes across it. Which is what Smith did, calling it the Anchor Bar, inspired by American naval prowess and, well, a lot of grog in an airport bar. The locals crucified him for it, but Smith is on a crusade undeterred.

"My business is wine but I make my life rougher by doing some of this other shit. I mean, I make over 200,000 cases of wine a year. So, if I make over $10 a case ... "

Which is his way of saying, put up or shut up.

"It keeps me busy. I'm not doing this other stuff for the money. I'm doing it because it's what I want to do. Turns out that it's work too. I want to contribute and do something. If it doesn't exist, stop complaining and do it yourself. I don't want to listen to anybody complain. So I said, screw it, I'll do it myself."

Smith's sounds like one of those stories that only happen in Danish fairytales. He got the girl, he got the millions, he's never lost the hair. When all's said and drunk, Smith will have had it his way—like

Sinatra, emerging from the pack, but more like Sid Vicious, all bloody and shitty, in skinny jeans and rock 'n' roll tees and riding Harleys to nowhere and back. If only you could bottle it, whatever's fueling him.

"The only problem is if your success implodes you and you become a jerk. You have to be willing to do everything and risk everything to do it. To thine own self be true. That's my thing."

Without my sense of taste, I would probably attempt to seek solace through other channels. I'd likely nibble on my boys' ears and let the laughter and the suppleness of young skin stand in for flavor. I'd kiss my wife harder, asserting strength over subtlety, which can be a healthy thing in such matters. I would stare out into space and seek redemption among the stars, imagining their white-hot flares and the unfathomable sear they would put on a flank steak, which with eyes closed and head pitched back I would hover inches over to see if I could at least feel the rhythms of the cinders beneath it, perceive the seasoning in a waft of steam. Thus senseless, I'd likely drown in the pools of blood and fat glistening on the surface, like a diamond necklace radiating on the bony white neck of a fallen queen that is first dispossessed of its charms and finally shorn from its body in order to satisfy the appetites, the tastes, of the insatiable mob.

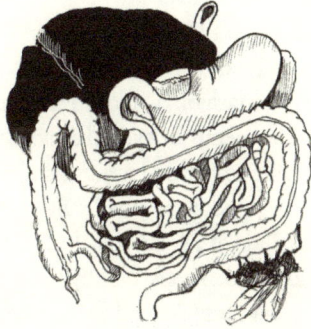

CHAPTER IX

THIS SIDE OF PARASITE

Uncle Doak would babysit us while my parents and their kin played cards and smoked cigarettes and drank coffee. He sat us with a scowl and a flyswatter. He died before I was out of pajamas, so I never saw his pleasant side. His death is to me more mystery than tragedy and over the years I have replayed the unswerving, thudding, late-braking sounds in my head as I imagined them to have played out in real time near the rise in road past Tannehill Cemetery over the hill from the state pen at McAlester. We buried my grandfather, Barney, next to Doak and moved on, my mother performing, with a gentle kiss on his waxen cheek, the final rite. So quick, so simple, so free of forms and estates and last wishes.

I hope to go somewhere in the middle. Not on the side of some country road, though probably not as blissfully as Barney, with a smell of fresh fish in a nose belatedly strung with last-gasp oxygen.

That'd be nice, but I think families only earn so many clean escapes, and Barney may have taken that cake.

I'm thinking by morsel would be fitting, to be undone by an edible. Say, a delicacy far out of fashion as food, preserved for purposes of antiquity but lost to the menus of even the most rich and infamous. A chicken, say, harboring something morbid under its skin. Or a fish bone: a shard of white slipped in on a tender flake. No doubt, if I get to choose, it'll be at the hands of a cook, somebody I trust, over a dish of something contraband and delicious. Not by treachery but complicity, for we'll both know what's at stake in the steak, what pearl of divinity the oyster has polished, or what poison lurks to inflict the diner who'd dare to go where many have gone but now don't dare because the FDA or the black market has darkened the path.

We never say, "You were what you ate."

Martyrs earn something for their trials. They earn at least our undying attempts—at remembrance, appraisal, rationalization, even respect. Attempts we muster to our own dying day.

Socrates drank the Senate's hemlock, which is said to have a "mousy" flavor, especially when bruised. (I knew a woman, an Australian, who tasted shit in a pinot grigio, for what it's worth.) Rasputin should have died of cyanide, laced in some cakes and wine, its taste of acrid almond silencing his formidable tongue. Big Jim Brady went to bed and never made breakfast. "Superinduced by acute indigestion," reads his obit in the *New York Times* of the heart attack that officially killed him. However acute the heartburn, it can't have been Diamond Jim's first bout. Brady was a grand gourmand, his haunts rich in culinary excess, his vast repasts well-documented: pair of ducks, three dozen oysters, six lobsters, a two-pound box of sweets, a few crabs, a sirloin, platters of accompanying vegetables. Nightly, the legend goes.

Not all poisonings are clandestine.

Exhibit A: Botulism Killed Them
Two Die of Rare Poison After Eating Cheese in a Salad
Special to *The New York Times* (August 2, 1914)

Los Angeles, Cal., Aug. 1—Two members of ojolly (sic) dinner party of seven, given last Sunday afternoon by Mrs. J. C. Cunningham of Ocean Park, have died from botulism, a peculiar form of ptomaine poisoning. The victims of the rare and slow working poison were Eugene Lettig of New York and Mrs. Emma De Ford of San Diego.

Mr. Lettig died yesterday at the home of his aunt, Miss D. Van Horn, 958 Sunbury Street. Mrs. De Ford died on Thursday. It is not known which of the foods served at the meal had the subtle poison, but the cheese in a salad is suspected.

Mr. Lettig and his mother, Mrs. J. C. Wood, came to Los Angeles last Fall for an extended visit. She returned to New York recently.

I don't keep a wish list of things to eat before I die; rather, as I die. The larder of life holds delicacies, reserving remedies for the apothecary. In other words, I've no interest in growing old on supplements. Rather, I have every interest in making my last meal a choice one. It doesn't have to be mammoth or comprehensive. (Unless it's wooly mammoth, defrosted from a dripping berg of black ice.) Selective and ripe will be the criteria, with an eye toward risk assessment but ultimately a blind one, turned instead into a glass of claret too dark for light to enter or escape. It will, this meal, certainly include cheese: room-temp, raw-milk, and crusty. A cheese that'll put hair on your chest, donated from its own overgrowth of fur and fuzz.

In fact, I have been felled by cheese three times. Once, it was a ripe, runny bleu d'Auvergne that came at the end of a slugfest involving salmon beurre blanc, coq au vin and three or so more courses. I'd eaten marathon meals before but never one chased with a cheese so veiny that it looked heroin-addicted. Twenty-four hours later, I was on the rack, with pains in the small of my back and a knot that my gut refused to swallow.

About a year later, pain came in the form of a fuzzy Saint-Marcellin whose warnings I ignored. You like a little mold on a Saint-Marcellin but mine was forced, acquired on the window sill of our Paris hotel. I closed my eyes as I ate, opening them between bites for views of the rainy Seine. I walked off the bridge, into the rain, none the worse for wear. On the train, I slept. The aches did not surface until we were safely back in the Languedoc. The following day, curled in bed and listening to harsh winds whip against the shutters, I let the mold run its course.

The first time: a bag of cheese popcorn. I inhaled it watching television and it owned me for hours afterward. My mother blamed it on the gorging, others the corn. I blame the cheese. Thirty-five years later and I can still taste it.

My bag of cheese popcorn was an uncouth act of youth. There is gluttony, and then there is just good taste. Dying to eat is not eating to die. There are basic differences, in form and function, that distinguish the glutton from the daredevil, the sloppy eater from the strategic. Not to mention the several shades of grey that cloud the diner's right to replenish or perish as he pleases. It isn't death I crave, it's flavor. But, as it happens, flavor tends to occur in the diciest of places.

Michael Paterniti, writing in *Esquire*, chronicled the last great supper of French President Francois Mitterand. As meals go, even French meals, it was a rich one, with oysters—their briny, bittersweetness surely evoking a bit of melancholy—leading off. It was the tamest of the four courses, followed as it was by sweetly dank goose liver and the spring capons, castrated for the president's dining pleasure. Then the ortolans. Is it enough to say they're forbidden by law or just mores? It's fitting that Francois, however wounded—more than once during the meal, he nearly fainted, apparently from exhaustion—chose to hold himself above the law of the land at his gorging-away table. Not unusual, really, in the realm of things (and certainly kings) for culinary opulence to trump legal standards.

You eat ortolans whole, your head veiled in a tented linen in order to keep the olfactory of steaming innards intact. Several of Mitterand's less-robust family members, it was reported, could be heard spitting bird brains and bones onto their plates. This mutiny can't have been music to his ears. Perhaps the fatigue or his own shroud impaired his hearing. Cacophonous or not, the meal would be his last. Eight days later, and with no other nourishment since the illegal bird, Mitterand expired.

The bell is always tolling, on life and consumption. With oysters, there must be a clock that alarms when allergy sets in. Or, in the case of my wife, a time bomb. There was a time she enjoyed oysters heartily. Then, we went to New Orleans for a long weekend and she enjoyed oysters as if and indeed for the last time. We ate them eight different ways, in as many locations, but the crushing blow was a single fried oyster at Mother's, glistening brown atop a pile of Tabasco-tinted grits. (I ate the other dozen or so, and all the grits.) She popped it and unknowingly ate her last decent mollusk. A year or so later, on Cape Cod, she found out the hard way that oysters weren't for her anymore. She found out again, even harder, over a shared order of moules-frites in Paris. That night, in our cramped room on the rue Cardinal Lemoine, she broke, swelling, sobbing, and fairly swooning onto the cold tile.

Exhibit B: Woman Dies After Eating Oysters
Posted: 8:18 am EDT September 11, 2007
WGCL TV, Atlanta

Fulton County health officials are advising people not to eat raw shellfish because it could be contaminated with a bacteria linked to the death of a woman who ate raw oysters at a restaurant in early August. The health department did not identify the woman, who died Aug. 10. She ate uncooked oysters several days before her death at a Spondivits restaurant.

[I surfed and found Spondivits home page recently. "Atlanta's Leader in Fine Seafood Served in a Casual Atmosphere Since 1979," it says up high on the page. "Great Food, Great Drinks, Great Fun!"

Another: "The only Atlanta bar pouring 2 oz+ drinks."

Finally, from Andy Camp, the owner, a testimonial: "There is no such thing as Perfection, but the great customers that walk through our doors really make us try harder."]

My own appetite for oysters is bound only by my stamina. In the era of paranoid eating that's come to regard the oyster with trepidation, I carry my weight. The one time they got the better of me they were not alone. It was a celebration among friends. I drank a martini at the bar as our communal table was being set. A colleague buoyed by the moment ordered me another. Instead of watering the plants with it, I drank it, or was drinking it when they called us to table. I'd just finished drinking it when the oysters arrived: a dozen Quilcene Bay beauties that I sucked bone dry.

Not long after, meat and wine appeared but something else went missing, namely my appetite and then my mind. At one point, lingering over a toast, I had to be talked back into my chair. I stared around the room at the dozen pals before me and became entranced by the collectiveness of their eating. It got warm all of a sudden. I was having trouble staying focused. The chop grew tepid on my plate, while in my stomach the oysters were making their run. By the time I hit the head, they were in battle roil. As they re-entered the earth's atmosphere—on a forceful slew of gastric juices that singed me from gullet to gum—I flipped my neck tie over my shoulder, closed my eyes, and swore I'd never mix gin and oysters again. An oyster needs no coaxing to cause trouble.

The sad fact is, I knew better, having read in a cookbook about the disastrous aspects of mixing oysters and spirits. This is, after all, a dish that brings combustibles with it. Oysters are "filter feeders," which means they suck in whatever soup's in the sea. Anymore, that's likely to be an ugly alchemy of industrial spillage and bacterial spew. Death by oyster is rare, nearly unheard of, but comes when it does in the cruelest fashion, often by dehydration (after incessant bouts of vomiting) and asphyxiation, brought on by paralysis of the muscles that control breathing. What's on the victim's mind, I wonder: a regret, a sadness, a song?

Foodborne illness sounds like something that floats in on the breeze, which in some cases I guess it does. The quaint "food poisoning" sounds alarmist by comparison. Protein is where it attacks. Beef, chicken, and eggs are the chief contaminants, but oysters always draw harsh light, probably because—unlike with raw chicken, raw cow, and, to an extent, raw eggs—oysters beg to be left uncooked. Preferring, even adoring, them fried, my dad won't touch a raw oyster. To spite him, in the beginning, and now through will and practice, I champion them raw. As with developing a taste for gin, it did not come easy this taste for oysters in their freshly dead condition. But it's mine now and for keeps.

What does all this learned flavor mean, these trials by fire and spice? I used to believe that it put me in a select company, at the high-risk end of an ill-fated group of eaters—gourmands all who by their practice and preference had become more susceptible than most to the ills of eating outrageous food. As an ethos, it wasn't hard to come by: All I had to do was eat. The wincing of those seated in my vicinity called my intentions into question, while doling out a potent measure of comeuppance. I ate the marrow, the sweetbreads, and the tripe, and that made me different. Any more, it makes you cool.

But the risky business of a radical appetite is not a belief system that holds up under scrutiny. In fact, it's bottom-feeding that's likely to do one in: the deli-case picnic salads slathered in mayonnaise, left to fester in the summer sun; the drive-through bacon cheeseburger with a scraping of bovine neural tissue accidentally ground in; the chicken nuggets that come 10 to a box—10 supercharged opportunities for a couple handfuls of known viral and bacterial infections. Consequently, absolutely, I don't eat that shit.

I tend to do the cooking in our house, so I can reduce the susceptibility to certain hazards by my shopping habits. It's no easy task anymore finding reliable, responsible sources for the most basic staples of the culinary minded carnivore. Meat, eggs, cheese, and milk are my Four Horsemen of the Apocalypse, riding herd no quarter and come to collect a final debt. The Sierra Club's Ken Midkiff[1] blames it on size in his small-farm directive, *The Meat You Eat*, even heading his chapters after the cash cows: Big Beef, Big Pig, Big Chicken (and Egg), Big Fish (a reference to all that salmon aquaculture we're now seeing).

---

1 "Their goal is uniformity of product," Midkiff writes of the fistful of companies that do the job once performed by thousands, "the better to maximize volume, efficiency, and the speed of the so-called disassembly line, where the cadavers are carved up." At the cost, Midkiff drives home, of stewardship, morality, and cleanliness, both environmental and food chain. Of course no cook, however clean, can eradicate contaminants. At best we can practice hygiene, trust our sources, and realize that sustenance is a dirty business. Lefkowitz is on the button. Life's omnipresent "mess" can be hell on the culinary arts.

After Thanksgiving, I poked around in the freezer case of doomed turkeys and found a frozen football labeled "hen." Forced to the corner by all the boneless breasts and Butterball blocks, it begged for an oven. But the first word I read on the plastic bag after "Hen" was "Injected," with smaller-type assurances of the "enhanced" flavor and juices to follow. And that was that. I dropped the bird and went and bought olives.

Statistically, in the realm of foodborne illness, you're nobody, until you get sick. Long ago, at a very glossy Chinese restaurant, I ate lamb and 24 hours later blamed it for my sweats and the searing stab in my midsection. After it passed, I was told to instead blame the rice. Rice breeds things, filthy enemies of the state of continence. Years later, though not too many, a friend of mine who waited tables at the place told me a story about tradition. A Chinese kitchen likes to keep the bones of its first butchered chicken, "for luck," he said. This particular restaurant framed its inaugural carcass, hanging it on the kitchen wall for posterity. When my friend entered the kitchen one morning and flipped on the light, he saw movement in the vicinity of dem bones. When he pulled back the picture frame, several roaches darted for cover. Presumably into a bucket of white rice.

Of all the things that could get you. Chinese cooks being frugal cooks—as all good ones are—you'd imagine the more hidden dainties to be the likeliest causes. Some nether part of the pig, or a mushroom cap sliced into a sour soup. To say nothing of the sea and all of its darker mysteries, secrets mastered by trained minds and tongues over the ages, but probably safer in China than in a refrigerated case thousands of miles west. Fermented, pickled and salty things, savories stewed and jarred in strange juices. Concepts to be feared, like duck eggs dangling in a stringy broth, thawing carp with eyes milkier than milt, caramelized duck carcasses glowing magenta beneath an infrared beam.

And the notorious MSG.

Good eating, even eating until you're so sick you want to die, doesn't cultivate a taste for death but of death. We do not savor the aged prime filet, the fermented fish, the creamy, veiny Roquefort for their freshness; rather, for their rotting genius—a sensation so nearly a flaw that it's taken centuries to perfect the process (of dry aging, say, or mold gathering) to prevent the carcass or the milk from rotting and dying instead of attaining enzymatic nirvana. Veering toward rotten and bordering on plain bad, these are the flavors of decadence. Eat them and you're tasting a near-death experience.

"As the ham comes in contact with your tongue, the punch of salt pushes forward," writes Peter Kaminsky in *Perfect Pig*, warming up to the famed, black, acorn-fed hog of Iberia. "Finally, as your teeth come together and you breathe out, you smell the return, only deeper, of that initial aroma of flesh and sweet decay." A heady perfume Kaminsky calls this experience, "just this side of rancidness." Even sexual, he states with a boldness typically reserved for the choicest erotica. "Most mammals," he concludes of the Spanish ham's pungency, "recognize it as a turn-on."

Be it the ham, the steak, a chunk of cheese, or an anchovy, the flavor of death, of sheer decadence, is the newfound fifth culinary sense—what the knowledgeable Japanese have for centuries labeled umami. And what all Asians (and my mother, in the form of a flavor enhancer called Accent, in a holiday cheeseball) have employed for ages under the label monosodium glutamate, or MSG.

By definition, a little MSG goes a long way. And a little is a good thing, eliminating as it does the reliance on salt in a savory dish. A dash of MSG, chemically, makes salt saltier, thus lessening the amount required. Employed with caution, it's an essential ingredient. (It naturally occurs all over the place—in balsamic vinegar, tomatoes, certain mushrooms and cheeses, kelp, soy beans, green tea. Bonita—dried, flaked, and sprinkled onto Asian greens—is umami through the roof, though for my tongue it reaches its apex in the form of fish sauce, a precursor of which was garum, a staple of the Roman empire. Garum was an intensely flavored paste with fermented fish as its backbone. The richer Romans ate it up. Fermented themselves, they must have required garum's savory inducement.)

In its twilight, Rome ate with all its might. Sensing the end, the gentry took the course of the glutton, hastening death one bite at a time. Kingdoms rise on the backs of labor and tumble in the bellies of the besotted. As declines go, Rome's took the cake, especially in the area of culinary opulence.

"Whether we regard the Augustan spendthrifts, or the later bon-vivants of the Eastern and Western Empires, it may be asserted that the Roman sensualist was devoid of nice perception," wrote British archivist John Cordy Jeaffreson, robbing Rome of its inalienable right. Twisting the dagger, he concluded: "Always a glutton, he was never an epicure in the modern sense of the term."

Sad, really. This is the civilization that created Apicius, who never met a lamb he didn't like. These are the farmers who planted vines in France. To go out powdering their drinks with pearls and favoring broiled birds not for their flavor but for their capacity to mimic human voice, this is plain suicide. However legendary, it's no legacy. Hell could be a toppled empire. To Rimbaud, hell was a cell. For me, hell is a tongue without a bud, no nose for aroma, an imbalanced brain, the organ where the wheelhouse of taste eternally resides.

Undaunted, flavor is a grail that leads the eater on through the ages, into ocean depths and beneath earthy hovels, on a restless quest. For some, the flavor of familiarity is enough. "Tastes good," as a sustaining mantra, suffices. Others tire of chewing the same old fat. A local restaurant chef once told me he'd lost his tongue for beef. "I've eaten too much of it," he said. "Anything tastes better to me than beef." He said this carving red slices from a slab of spit-roasted goat.

Godzilla rose from the Sea of Japan, whetted I guess on a gargantuan platter of freshest sashimi and hungry for something inland. Conversely, in the heartland, we eat from the inside out, sating ourselves on steak and spuds and only occasionally satisfying a hankering for other flesh. We turn to the sea out of hunger—for something different, something not meat—and then beat a retreat. We are all monsters, pissed at the sameness of place and staples, pulled by a craving.

Sushi came to the middle of nowhere, I'm convinced, to kill me. The proprietors Fed-X their fish in, assuring us of freshness.

However fashionably Asian the young chefs, I can't help but sense the absurdity of eating raw fish this far inland, with no hint of sea air about, only cologne, climate control, electronica, and cocktails preserving the hipness and compounding the confusion. I can't doubt that the fish is fresh, not and eat it. But then, I note, most around me are eating tempura, miso soup, and fishless-sushi rolls named for local pop bands and trendy avenues. They are ordering, of all things, steak.

And so it occurs to me—with a slimy tail of raw shrimp filming my teeth and barely enough wasabi to go around—that I will be done in by red meat.

In a famously stark scene from *Soylent Green*—to my taste, Charlton Heston's finest moment—a full-lipped Leigh-Taylor Young bribes Chuck with her choicest victuals: a ripe, red piece of steak hanging by a hook. The year was 2022 ("New York City. Population: 44,000,000.") and all meat beyond reach.

It might be outstripped supply or it might be spongiform but the demise of beef can't be far off. In *Soylent Green*, a more predictable protein source for the masses became a necessity and, in the hands of "Saturday Night Live," a punchline. In more enlightened cultures, the purpose of beef was never to anchor white china dimmed by candlelight. Meat's too dear for that. Steak as chop simply can't be with us forever. Naturally, the closer it gets to rarity—meaning, the more less of us eat it on anything resembling a regular basis—the higher the opportunity for calamity.

Already, the hour is upon us. On the nightly news, another story of beef recall washed across the screen in a wave of freshly ground round. As surgically capped and gowned factory workers sterilized tile walls, another carted the bad blood off to the Dumpster. Before breaking for a commercial, our local anchor teased us with a video clip of a bank heist. "When we come back," he promised.

Exhibit C: Chokes to Death Eating Meat
Pittsburg, Penn., Jan. 30—A dozen foreigners discussed

the meat boycott at breakfast in a Mulberry Alley boarding house to-day, and all except "Mic" Skovlac agreed to eat no meat. Skovlac, delighted with having the breakfast steak to himself, tackled it so violently that he choked to death with the first mouthful.

The New York Times, January 31, 1910

At a two-star lunch in Lyon, I opted for the bucolic "*Trois jolie plats.*" Three pretty plates, indeed, one of them a dish that translates roughly to "suckling lamb pulled from beneath its mother." It was served on a bed of grains, its juices moistening the food it never had a chance to grow fat on. I ate the fated beauty not yet a beast because I am a weak man and this is what I do.

In a filthy documentary called *Le Sang des betes* (The Blood of the Beasts), director George Franju saves a slew of young lambs for his money shot. It's a nearly balletic symphony of blood, reflexes, and aberration. Runner up: A horse being slaughtered by a former pugilist hobbling on a stump. (He'd severed an artery in his thigh with a filet knife years before.) Grinning through a Galoise, the middleweight stun-gunned a white horse the way he must have once jabbed an opponent. Watching the horse buckle to its knees was like seeing Jack Kennedy's head snap back in the Zapruder reel.

I saw *Le Sang* after watching Franju's *Eyes Without a Face,* a gorgeous film about a mad scientist who steals pretty girls from Paris, carts them to his chateau in the outskirts, drugs them, then scalpels their faces as cleanly as possible in order to create a new visage for his daughter whose beauty was ruined in a car crash. *Le Sang des betes* is a bonus feature on the DVD release.

Clearly, I am bound by meat, made of it, have a taste for it so developed that, like my chef friend, I require the tang of age and near rottenness in order to eat beef with any relish (or without dissolving it in a slow-cooked gravy of wine, or a bowl of pho, where its bones and tissues have been bled of all their savor to make a broth of the beefiest flavor ever). And so meat it will be, if not ground round then aged prime, cut off the back of the beast by a boxer with a bad leg. It simply has to be.

I am pulled to the flavor of the animal, to the blood of the lamb. For a last supper, I could ask no more. Perhaps some potatoes, twice-fried and crispy, and by any means wine— like the Mourvedre I recently drank to chase a medium-rare Chateaubriand. Grapy, ghostly, almost floral, and with a preposterous taste of freshly dug earth.

Before he developed a spot on his lung, my dad smoked Winston Lights. Before that and for years he smoked full-on Winstons. He was not alone. For three or four years on both sides of the '70s, Winstons were one of the top brands in America. These were prime smoking years for my dad—and my mom, too—this turbulent era of Prague and Chicago and Munich and Bobby Kennedy. "Winston tastes good," the tagline went, "like a cigarette should." I Googled Winston and it Googles, as you'd imagine, pretty high (meaning ahead of Churchill and Winston-Salem, its namesake). But you have to click on "winston cigarettes" to get to the R.J. Reynolds site, which looks nothing like the home page of a tobacco purveyor. More like one of those companies you can't quite make out what they sell. "We are ... principled, creative, dynamic and passionate." Back in the day, apparently, Winston was the number one brand in Puerto Rico, where an aunt and uncle of mine spent some time. They brought back no duty-free Winstons but, rather, fresh pineapples and coconuts and a wooden bowl that I now serve salad out of sometimes.

CHAPTER X

OF SPICE AND MEN

T hey reported his demise in the Tulsa Daily World on 10 November 1928.[1] Ike, more proprietor than legend in '28, did not merit front-page news. Front page that day, the explosion of Etna: "Second Village Falls Prey to Devouring Lava." In fact, Ike's stroke made bigger headlines than his death. Over his one-column portrait are set the words, "Paralysis Victim," as if Ike were its poster child.

The *Tulsa Tribune*, a day earlier and with more vigor, put his demise on page 20, in its "Market News" section. It also wrote its headlines in upper and lower case, another element of style:

Ike Johnson, 70, of Chilli Fame, Is Ill With Paralysis
Stricken as He Started to Board Bus and Condition Critical

However written, the end was swift. Both papers had it in their

---

1 Associated Press style would dictate the 10 follow the November, with a comma before the year. But I have always preferred Strunk and White's suggestion. The key, as any good copy editor will tell you, is consistency.

November 12 editions. The *World*:

'IKE' JOHNSON, PIONEER, DEAD
Man Who Gained Name of 'Chili King' in Tulsa Dies at 69

The Ike now bracketed in single quotes. Ike may not have been a front-page item, but he was still an institution and familiar enough in all of Tulsa's small circles to go by his nickname. And in the *Trib*, with one less "L" in chili than in earlier editions:

Ike Johnson, Famed as Chili Maker, Is Dead
Body to Lie in State Today; Burial in Texas

From whence he came, a sweet spot not far over the Red River called Honey Grove. Ike landed in Tulsa in 1907, the year of statehood, and found work in a restaurant he would own within a year.

"Uncle Ike is one of the most enthusiastic boosters Tulsa ever had," reads a quote in his obit, attributed to "his nephews." "He always was the first to defend Tulsa against any criticism."

I've looked for Ike in photos of The 100, that group of commercial showmen who boared a train headed east to tout the doin's in boomtown Tulsa for audiences in whatever cities would entertain them. If he's in there, I didn't find him, bobbing in the sea of similarly old, white, bald guys. That note of coming to Tulsa's defense in the quote, that's another of the city's legacies.

The first Ike's chili wasn't served in an Ike's but in a joint "in the north alley between Main and Boston" that Ike bought from one Frank Morris. That was 1908. A year later, Ike reopened at 119 S. Boston Ave., mere steps away in the Reeder Building, with the focus now solidly on chili. Over the next quarter century, all of Ike's five nephews—Ivan O., Mortimer T., Carl, Henry and William Preston—at least dabbled in the chili business.

Ike was stricken on a train platform, heading to Pawhuska on another of his land deals, said Selma Johnson, the centenarian widow of William Preston ("W.P." from here on). Ike poked across the southwest in search of oil. Chili became his black gold, in legend if not ledgers. He died a year before the big crash a single man, which he'd remained his entire life. "But he always had a friend with him," Selma said. "He called them his companions." Men still died with their boots on in those days, and often not in hospitals. Isaac "Ike" Johnson died at his home, 415 E. 15th St., where he lived with brother Preston Brooks Johnson and nephew W.P.

I drove by this address in vain. Whatever house was there gave up the ghost for the Inner-Dispersal Loop built in the late 1960s and took out a slice of Tulsa known as Little Bohemia. The former Johnson residence is now an "Up With Trees" plot, between the Broken Arrow Expressway and Maple Park.

Chili, however you spell it, came out of the land of scrub and hoof, up from Coahuila in the Mexican plain into the vast triangulation of Abilene, San Antonio and Chihuahua, where a lot of miles and men and beasts crossed paths on the way to slaughter. Men rode herd with chili in their guts, wiping the grease from their hands into their hair and beards.

Chiles—guajillo, ancho, pasilla and the like—dried like a charm, as did the fresh-killed beef. Reconstituted, they made a stew of the most peppery sort. Beans are a latter-day addition apparently, though their ability to dry nicely would seem to make them ready kin for the chili pot. Whatever, beans have no place in so-called "Texas chili." San Antonio claims the dish but who wouldn't have a stake in claiming chili? The legendary "chili queens" of San Antone, hawkers of street-corner "bowls of red," simply put a face on a pastime. A kind of Dallas Cowboy cheerleader with a ladle.

It isn't clear if he met him here or brought him north, but very soon in his chili experiments Ike Johnson teamed up with one Alex Garcia, who must have known a thing or two about chili.

"They had a Mexican," Zurn Johnson, another nephew, told me in 2004, "and he had a recipe that would set you free."

Together, reads a mimeographed family history, Ike and Alex "worked out" a recipe that has survived wars, drought, shortage, marketing chutzpah, and all sorts of family heresy. Garcia, reads an afterthought, "was of Spanish descent."

Ike and Ivan went about smoothing out the recipe's rough edges, suiting it to a Tulsan's taste, which in 1910 apparently veered toward the tame. "They toned it down," Zurn said, "because it would set you on fire. They felt like they'd come up with something pretty good, so he closed down his family restaurant and opened a chili place at Second and Main. Without a name."

Harry Sinclair came to Tulsa in 1905, the year they struck on Ida Glenn's farm, a rich enough pool to name a town after (Glenpool, minus an "n"). Soon after, Standard Oil started laying pipelines. Wells there produced 1000 to 3000 barrels a day. By 1906, 8000 acres were developed. "Wildcat" was a reference to drilling where no man but only beast roams.

In 1911, the Supreme Court of the United States busted the trust of Rockefeller's Standard Oil, opening the flood gates. Drillers arrived in droves. By 1913, 25,000 barrels a day were flowing from wells at Cushing. Bartlesville followed: Osage elders leased vast acreages and established rich trusts.

In 1911, Mortimer and Ivan open a chili parlor in Kansas City that closed within the year. In 1911, Tom Slick, as wild a cat as ever was, came to Cushing to stake his claim.

Ike went on sabbatical soon after, first to New Mexico, where according to Selma Johnson he visited family and rested. Then onto Tulia, halfway between Amarillo and Lubbock, where Ike had once bought land. Something took him back to Tulsa but it wasn't chili. "He was out of the business by 1913," Selma said, "but he always had his finger on it. He was very protective of the name 'Parlor.'"

In 1996, the First Presbyterians of Boston Avenue bought the old Masonic Lodge, where Ike's had a groundfloor eatery. William Harvey Johnson ("W.H.") had been keeping Uncle Ike's namesake alive there since 1959—in hindsight, a year of infamy—but church needs had outgrown those of chili at 712 S. Boston Ave.

"I grew up downtown," W.H. told *Tulsa World* columnist Terrell Lester, who wrote a column on the closing. "I mean

I literally grew up down there on Third Street," a reference to another shop, the same one that a rejuvenated Ike opened with his nephew Ivan Oliver Johnson ("I.O.") in 1915 at 312 S. Main St. There, a "Three in One"—chili, beans and spaghetti—ran you 15 cents. Cincinnati, which claims the three-way, also cooks a "five-way," laying on chopped onions and gobs of orange cheese.

"That three-way term is our term," Zurn once argued.

Back when they had a shop on 11th Street, near the university, Selma and W.P. would be walking across a parking lot and somebody would yell out, "Hey! How about a three-way?"

In 1912, Carl and a man named Klein bought Ike's place at 119 South Boston. In 1913, they moved the parlor one door north to number 117. Two years later, Ike returned from Tulia and opened a new shop with Ivan. Zurn recalled:

"'Why don't you call it Ivan's Chili,' somebody said. Well, Ivan was too shy. But Ike was out of town. My grandfather said, OK, then painted Ike's name on the front window. He kept an eye out for Ike.

"Sure enough, when he came in from the field ... You know those really big pipe wrenches they use on a rig? Well, Ivan said he'd throw Ike in right after it, and Ike believed him."

Oil rigs rose out of the blackened landscape like naked tree trunks in a big-acre burn. Speculation and skullduggery went unchecked. Tulsa, which should have grown up by now, has sucked on the tit of big oil ever since.

Prospectors named their firms in hopes of hits: Clover Leaf, Hoppy Toad, Ideal, Only, Future, Success, Invincible, Midnight Oil. Oil settlements popped up, veering right: Gasright, Downright, Alright, Damright, Justright, Dropright. My dad's dad landed in Drumright[2], cranking a wrench for Pure Oil.

Ike's Chili boomed at a time when the whole of the Tulsa restaurant scene was confined to a few city blocks. The diners

---

2 The scene inspired one F.S. Barde, the Oklahoma correspondent of the *Kansas City Star*: "... any man with a gill of red blood in him is stricken immediately with the oil fever upon reaching Drumright. He begins seeing things grow larger and larger at every turn. He is soon talking in terms of thousands where a day earlier the best he could do was about two bits. The atmosphere is charged with superlatives and hyperbole."

and cafes[3] were in bed with each other, sharing alley space and swapping spit. Most of them had a chili recipe. Chili was the lubricant that kept the ill-fed, hung-over, sleep-starved, oil-field itinerants from floating off in a haze of fumes.

In 1926, Mortimer Johnson opened an Ike's Chili Parlor on Fourth Street, in the Oklahoma Union Railroad Transportation Building. In 1927, Carl sold his Boston Avenue shop to Wayne Foster, a family friend, who after a few months dropped the Ike's name in favor of Foster's Chili. Millard Johnson, a cousin, worked for Foster until 1930. In 1929, Mortimer closed the Fourth Street shop. In 1930, Ivan and W.P. bought his equipment and went into business at 111 South Boston as Ike's Chili II. The family tree, already sagging under its many branches, began to crack.

William Zurn Johnson squeezed into a wooden school chair, its stressed lumber squeaking beneath him. He poured me a cup of coffee into a mug silk-screened with an "Evan's Bail Bonds" logo. He pushed a bowl of creamer toward me.

"I can do black," I said.

Zurn looked up from his own pour. "You sure? I use this," he said, showing me a half-gallon of cream. His own coffee—now the color of Vanessa Williams—he drank from a Styrofoam bowl that typically holds a small chili-to-go. He took oxygen through a slender tube from a tank marked "Lincare: The caring choice." Zurn spoke carefully, considerately. He worked on his coffee some more.

"I'm not quite awake yet," he said.

Wallpaper depicting stuffed library stacks of the foregone classics rims the walls at Ike's on Admiral, the only Ike's left. Zurn Johnson ran the place, cooked the chili, minded the store for his dad, W.H., who was housebound a decade before his death in 2007.

---

3   "One entrepreneur," wrote Ruth Sheldon Knowles in *The Greatest Gamblers*, "arriving with a $42 stake opened a restaurant not much bigger than a cigar box. Serving clean, well-prepared food, he made a $500 profit in a week. He eventually made more of a fortune from the oil in his cook stove than the majority of those who were bringing it up from the ground."

Ike's made a downtown comeback in 2002, at Fifth and Main, but it lasted less than a year. Zurn blamed it on the restructuring of the Main Mall from pedestrian byway to drivable thoroughfare. Ike's closed its doors "amid all the traffic and carpet bombing."

A photo on the wall depicting one of the many old parlors shows a portion of the hand-lettered sign, with "Chilli" getting the twin Ls of the Nahuatl spoken by the Aztecs, or maybe it was a misprint, the one that misled the *Tribune* headline writers. I was about to inquire when Zurn awakened in a burst.

"Dudn't matter! I'm working on another deal anyway."

Inspired by a History Channel story on a Texas diner called The Pig Stand and the beginning of drive-thru service, Zurn went to plotting. "It increased business 30 to 36 percent. That got my attention. That's the bottom line for me."

I imagined drive-thru chili and all the spoon-fed collision likely to ensue. Less ambitiously, Zurn also had an idea for a new seasoning mix. W.P., W.H.'s uncle and nemesis, preferred the spice made famous by Willie Gebhardt of New Braunfels, Texas. I'd learned that from Selma, I told him.

"Ah ..." Zurn sort of gasped. "W.P. worked for Ivan. Then he went off to the Great War and fought with the Doughboys. When he came home, he asked for his old job back. Then he very quietly snuck around and opened the location at 36th and Harvard.

"He did an end run on 'em."

A small, gold slip of paper jumps out of the *Tulsa World* "Ike's Chili Parlor" clip file. In parlance, it is called a "kill." It's dated 13 Nov 1959 and composed in mid-century, manual typewriter hieroglyphics: lots of quick hyphens, clunky underlines, letters nudging each other and others kerned far apart—like teeth in a head missing a few—and a heaviness in places where the writer meant to really hammer home a thought.

The miscues are smashed over with a bunch of Xs. I've cleaned it up here, but the intent of the message will remain a mystery:

"Following actions taken this date at the personal request of
Walter Ahlum:"

"Killed--

Two   3-col cuts of interior of old West Third Street restaurant

One   2-col cut of W.H. and Joseph M. Johnson receiving
chili recipe from father, I.O."

"Virgil D. Curry, Librarian"

Walter Ahlum also wrote for the *Tulsa Democrat* where,
he confessed in a 1950s column, "My instructions were one
legitimate local item to four faked ones, very easy to conceal
because the town was growing so rapidly that few people
knew each other."

"Cuts" are references to photographs. "Kill" means file and
never print again.

"I remember it pretty well," Zurn recalled in 2004 and on his
last legs. "It was '59 so, let's see, I was 11. And I was mad as
hell. I was the one who advocated a lawsuit. To me, the brutal fact
was the sneaky way it was done."

A kid appeared from the kitchen and set a plate down in
front of Zurn. On it were four pancakes swimming in syrup
saddled with six strips of bacon, which Zurn pushed off onto
the placemat to make room.

"They're apple this time, instead of banana," said the cook. "I
didn't have any banana. Anything else?"

"No," Zurn said. "Yes! Whipped cream. And I could use a fork."

The guy hurried out and returned with a pastry bag for piping
cream. Zurn swirled a big snake of it onto his cakes.

"Would you mind getting me a glass of milk, thank you."

Then he eyeballed me wildly as if he'd forgotten I was there.

"There were other signs," he said. "I could see it coming. But I
don't mean to sound clairvoyant. What irks me is, I'd get phonecalls.
'What the hell's with that chili on Harvard!' I remember it being
lighter in color. And the flavor, it just didn't taste the same.

"It makes me mad when I get chewed out for something I didn't do. Pride, I guess."

I rose to leave an hour later and, for the first time, noticed Zurn's T-shirt. "Chili ... and a little bit more," it read.

Chili greases both sides of the spoon, of course. I went to Burgundy Place, out near the old City of Faith, to get Selma's.

"I don't want to get into the family deal," she said but we do anyway. What happened in 1959 was this:

"Our son came out of college and, um, when Ivan's son (W.H.) got into the business there was a little difference of opinion about this and that. My husband wanted to keep the 'Chili Parlor' name and Ivan and his son, Bill, thought 'Chili House' was more appropriate for the times.

"Our son went into business out on South Harvard."

One night there, a Coke machine blew up from carbonation overload. "Thank God we were closed," Robert Johnson said. The scrapbook photos show a toppled container and a black spot on the floor, as if the IRA had suddenly taken an interest in the politics of chili.

"When we opened the chili parlor on Harvard," said Selma, "we cooked it the same way that Uncle Ike cooked it—on a gas stove with three burners for three vats that each held 50 pounds of chili meat.

"Of course, today meat is not the same."[4]

Selma paused for me to catch up in my notes.

"My husband continued to use Gebhardt's chili powder. There were just different little things that my husband liked to do. In fact, he was the one who'd measure the spice and see that it got cooked properly. He was the younger brother and sort of took over. He wasn't married at the time, not until 33."

Selma, fresh from a stint at Miss DeHaven's flower shop, married into the chili business.

---

4 "Grain feeding took off in America after World War II," reads the introduction to *The Niman Ranch Cookbook* (Bill Niman and Janet Fletcher, 2005, Ten Speed Press). "With the country at peace, many wartime gunpowder factories converted to fertilizer production, boosting the use of these chemicals in American agriculture." Corn production skyrocketed, the argument goes, and fueled the era of corn-fed cattle. By contrast, various small-farm operations—and some, like Niman Ranch, not so small—have taken to letting cattle graze in pastures rather than fatten in feedlots. The twin camps of corn-fed marbling and grass-fed richness now stand their opposing grounds.

"I didn't come into the family until 1933. Of course, that's a sore spot. This younger generation had all sorts of other ideas."

In 1942, Vera Jackson and Pat Rogers donned the aprons of Ike's Chili, the first women ever to do so. In 1950, W.H. and Joseph M., twins sons of Ivan O., opened Ike's Suburban, 2413 E. Admiral Place, in Whittier Square. In 1954, W.H. began wholesaling Ike's frozen chili to local markets, perhaps with a little press payola. "After a long, hard day's work," one story began, "this reporter decided to treat herself to a delicious dinner and maybe a few drinks at Ike's."

In 1966, Zurn left Tulsa for Tulane. In 1970, he went to work at Brennan's, one of New Orleans' older houses. "That's where I learned to do bananas Foster. And specialty drinks. The Bluetail Fly, which was cream of cacao, cream and blue curaçao. You shake it all up and serve it in a tall glass. It was a very good drink. And one with bananas, too ... I forget."

In 1972, Zurn and W.H. acquired The Forge from Grant Hastings, who'd stuck a big fireplace in the middle of the room and grilled, on his own Hasty-Bake "charcoal ovens," burgers and steaks, plus game brought in by fellow hunters. Zurn lit up at the memory of it. "Oak tables, oak chairs, oak booths and an oak bar. I said, 'We need to serve more than just chili here.' "

Zurn and his dad were sitting around one evening, trying to come up with a name for the place. W.H.'s tongue tied up and out came, "Now, about this atmosfood..." Zurn alone, it seems, liked the way it sounded. "People didn't get it," he said. "And they were looking for Ike's, which means chili."

So they changed it. Ike's Atmosfood became Chez Ike, a suggestion blurted out one night by a sufficiently impressed diner. "We were doing trout meuniere l'amandine, filets du poisson en soufflé, escargots champignon. That was a good one. It wasn't expensive, compared with today's prices. But people were having a hard time understanding the concept. It smacked of the French thing. At that time, Tulsa was a beef and taters kind of town."

There may have been more to do with the naming of Chez Ike than guerilla marketing. In September 1972, W.H. sued W.P. and

Robert over trademark usage. The suit was tossed from district court when it became clear that the secretary of state's office had issued identical trademarks to both parties. W.H., then doing business as Ike's Chili House, let his trademark expire. It was then issued to W.P., who was calling his place Ike's Chili Parlor. Said the court: "When the trademark expired in 1970, both sides in the dispute apparently applied for renewal, leading to the fuss over rights to the name."

William Harvey Johnson, son of Ivan Oliver, died at age 84 two days after Christmas of 2007. His son, William Zurn, went in May of '08, taking with him the Johnson name if not the legacy. "He was a stickler for perfection—he took the chili very seriously. It was almost a religious experience to him."

So said Zurn's stepson, Chris Trail, in his dad's obit. Trail runs the last remaining Ike's Chili House, the one at 5941 E. Admiral Place, where four years before Zurn and I drank coffee. Trail is the keeper of the recipe Zurn got from William Harvey, the one that "ain't wrote down," Zurn told me in 2001.

Before the 2002 economy drove them out, Chris Trail got his wish, to bring Ike's back downtown. Its painted windows still stand in the vacant first floor space of the Sinclair Building. Trail ran for City Council in 2009 and represented the 5th District until 2011.

"You'll see businessmen sitting next to guys from American Airlines," Zurn said during my last visit to Ike's. I saw an American Indian walk by delivering soft drinks.

At age 26, Tom Slick sold all of his Cushing holdings for $2 million. Seventeen years later, he sold all he'd amassed again for $35 million. Slick, the darling of Cushing, died in 1930, at 46, overworked.

Ivan O. Johnson shot himself somewhere in his home at 1220 E. 17th Place on 27 October 1966. "A revolver lay near Mr. Johnson's body," the *Tribune* reported. "County Investigator Claude Davis ruled the death an apparent suicide." A recent cataract surgery had left him "despondent," relatives were quoted.

The press clipping isn't marked "Tribune," but Hilary Pittman, the *Tulsa World* librarian and arguably its greatest asset, could tell by the clues: the use of "today" in the lead (the *World*, being a morning paper, would have written "yesterday"), a teaser to Jim Downing's column on the back side of the clipping, and by the serif headline font.

You have to read to the fifth paragraph to find out that I.O. and W.H. were mere days away from opening the shop out on Admiral. "Opening of this restaurant was postponed today because of the senior partner's death." Johnson died on Thursday. The Admiral shop was to have opened Monday. Again, it is the last left standing.

I drove by the house, just south of B'nai Emunah synagogue, a few years ago and found it for sale. I e-mailed the broker to arrange a viewing but never got a reply. The house finally sold.

Until I met Darrell Merrell, the self-proclaimed "Tomato Man with Garlic Breath," garlic was white and tomatoes were red. But in the realm of heirloom gardening and husbandry, the colors are less set. From a back acre of tomato vines he'd lost time and track of, I filled baskets full of rare, sun-split beauties: Green Zebra, Black Cherry and Cherokee Purple, his pick of the litter. His garlics were likewise loud and proud: Persian Star, German Extra Hardy, Inchelium Red, Spanish Roja. Then, after garlic ennui set in, he started gathering up mail-order chickens: Welsummers and Barnevelders, Cherry Eggers and Barred Rock, Red Dorking and Buff Orphington, which rang to me of Ivy League frat boys. He was writing an encyclopedia in his mind. Such projects, of course, are bigger than men. Even Merrell, a towering Burl Ives in blue overalls until the cancer got him. One fan, back for his annual tomato plants, wept when he heard the news. I think of the seed those tears might have sprouted underfoot.

CHAPTER XI

AN ODE TO THE CLOVE

My mother the cook was raised in the Canadian River bottoms, in the shadow of coal-mining Krebs and its passel of mom-and-pop pasta houses—Isle of Capri, Pete's Place, Roseanna's, Gia Como's—but far enough removed to skirt the aromas. My father, an eater who grows contentious over bloody meat, crisp vegetables and fish that isn't fried, flees garlic faster than the undead. Thus, the savage clove had no place in our home. I had to move out to embrace it in earnest.

The first time I cooked with garlic, where it called for one clove I chopped up the whole ball of twine, mistaking a head (or bulb) for a clove. In cooking, it takes experience for the terms of art to reveal themselves and unravel their mysteries. It took me forever to stop lifting the protein too early from the sauté pan, and to quit hunting the Homeland aisles for arrowroot.

Garlic, like anything dear, needs handling to be loved and understood. Stripping away the outer paper is like undressing a body, each layer exposing more of the firmness and shape of the skin within. Peel back enough layers and you embrace a curve, smooth and ivory, depending on the varietal. The cloves nestle to the neck, if it is a hardneck, clinging to the roots at the basal plate. A clove is smooth, firm and pointed, like the polished toe of a cloven-hoofed beast.

I read in *Spin* a long time ago that the Pogues' Shane Macgowan staved off colds by eating raw garlic and starvation with tiramisu. Another punk, the absinthe-logged poster boy of Montmartre named Henri de Toulouse-Lautrec, is from neither Toulouse nor Lautrec. He is from Albi, where we get Albigensian, as in the crusades that racked the band of 13th-century heretics called Cathars. Lautrec is the home of a garlic whose cloves are compact and juicy and mammoth. A head of Lautrec is as big as a rabbit's. Toulouse, France's fourth largest city, is an ancient place legendary for religious turmoil, rocket science, and garlic sausage, with much else to offer in between. In the southwest, where the cooking is more rustic, Toulouse and its sausage add backbone to a classic cassoulet.

There is little paper on a bulb of Lautrec, a hardneck variety that renders roughly ten cloves a head. The color is pink, hence the name *ail rose*. Peeling a clove of it is like unwrapping a piece of hard candy.

My 1961 edition of *Larousse Gastronomique* devotes as many paragraphs to garlic as curative as it does recipes, quoting the likes of Virgil, Aristophanes, Celsius and Mohammed. "In Cayenne garlic is used against bites of certain snakes." About as enticing as it gets in the kitchen is garlic toast; about as obvious is garlic oil: "This oil is used for seasoning salads."

In things temporal, *Larousse* is my bible. Its pages highlight the lives of the gastric saints—Careme, Brillat-Savarin, Escoffier, Taillevent—and its gospel of definitions guides me on my culinary voyage. But the good book's lack of depth on garlic makes me wonder if the topic resides in some lost apocrypha that I'll one day stumble upon.

For a nation so intent on writing the history of cooking, it seems strange to be so wholly devoted to garlic's remedial value so late in the game. On page 445, smack in the heart of the great canon—a mere four entries from "gastronome" itself—garlic snoozes between the garden warbler and a fussy list of garnishes. Above it, hiding wisely, is the threatening, three-line entry for:

garfish (Snipe eel). *Orphie*—The garfish, or sea eel, has dry, lean flesh, poisonous at certain times. Prepare like Conger eel (see EEL).

Or don't.

I can only believe that garlic is, was, and ever shall be so obvious to the cooking of France that it goes without saying even in *Larousse*. Garlic is a given, an element whose inclusion is accepted on faith and need not be chronicled to be believed.

Either way, Paula Wolfert makes amends in *The Cooking of Southwest France*, her painfully authentic anthem to the regions of Perigord and Languedoc, where a special note on garlic is sandwiched between "The Fats of the Southwest" and "Bayonne Ham." Chopping versus crushing, Wolfert argues, releases less sulphur and acid and steadies garlic's overpowering tendencies. Primo argues likewise in the film *Big Night*, instructing baby brother Secundo not to chop too finely lest all you taste is garlic.

Garlic is inescapable in these recipes, from the two heads in Chicken with Garlic Pearls in Sauternes—where the whole cloves caramelize in the sweet wine—to the half clove rubbed on the inside of a dish of Auvergne potato gratin. In the region situated below Bordeaux, Wolfert has found food with body, soul and multiple cloves.

When I have pistachios, and I never do, and if I remember, and I never do, I love to make Chester's Favorite Roasted Garlic-Pistachio Pasta, which combines minced parsley, chicken stock, olive oil, toasted pistachios (some whole, others ground to thicken the sauce) and two heads of Duganskij garlic, a courageous one head per serving.

You'll likely be making this, if you make it, without Duganskij, a Czech breed among the 32 varieties of garlic from 17 nations, part of the garden of Chester Aaron. He has a particular fondness for Tochliavari, of Georgian origin, as is Chester. What he calls

Russian Red Toch. (I knew a guy out on 11th Street who sold bags with names like Russian Red Toch. A yellow light glowed over his card-table kitchen. A television blinked in muted silence. I knew him through a friend of a friend and we only went out there once. She conducted her business and I stayed out of the way, in the dark, widening my degrees of separation.)

In Occidental, up the coast from San Francisco—and at the opposite end of the bay from Gilroy, "Garlic Capital of the World"—Aaron defies the garlics foisted on the supermarkets. Not until reading his book did I realize I was being cheated, and not until I met Darrell Merrell did I read Chester Aaron's *Garlic is Life*, Chester's homage to anything but the papery bulbs of Gilroy, those heads full of little spindly cloves that fall out like baby teeth.

A n interest in garlic and deadlines led me to Al Sadavandi, who was running a place on Boulder Avenue called the Garlic Grill. I'd just written a story about French fries. Garlic seemed a solid next step. I was going to knock off my favorite edibles one byline at a time. Sensing I was after more than a few quotes, Al called in his buddy Darrell, an heirloom gardener with a business card read.

We sat in the carpeted dining room, in the post-lunch lull, with the smells of garlic, onions and oil caramelizing in steel troughs of marinara. Darrell wore a thick, red beard and a set of faded overalls. He was a robust man who confessed to throwing a fistful of garlic cloves into whatever he happened to be cooking. Al was a Tulsa restaurant veteran with a Rat Packer's enthusiasm for the table. I assumed he was Italian, but I asked anyway.

"I am ... Persian," he said, grinning as if he'd eaten a small bird.

This was in the winter of 2001, several months before being of Middle Eastern descent raised flags. A broad map of the swath above the Sinai Peninsula spread out across my brain. I opened my mouth to speak but, before I put my foot in it, Darrell said, "Al's Iranian. Now ... he doesn't promote that."

We talked for a good hour and a half, which left me with a pile of chicken-scratch notes to decipher. On my way out the door, Darrell gave me a dozen brown lunch sacks of garlics with big-ass names like

Spanish Roja, Polish Carpathian and Georgian Crystal. All were grown on his farm just off of US 75 southwest of town. Where Aaron had honed his lot of varieties to under three dozen, Merrell was at a robust 365 and counting—likely downward since his goal was to plant a host of varieties and whittle down to the hardiest.

Inside each bag were six to eight heads, some of them with cloves the size of Brazil nuts. He also gave me a book, *Sauer's Herbal Cures*, first compiled by Johann Christopher Sauer from 1762 to 1778, with Pennsylvania food historian William Woys Weaver doing the translating, editing and updating. Occasionally over supper I will pull Sauer off the shelf and read something at random. It's a cheap shot to include it here, but the man's message regarding garlic is no-holds-barred, even for colonial America:

> "Garlic is employed in cookery and medicine. It warms and dries a cool, moist stomach, kills and expels worms, and helps against the bites of snakes and mad dogs. If garlic is eaten and worn outwardly, rats and other noxious creatures will flee from it. If a snake or lizard should crawl into the stomach of someone during sleep, that person should eat garlic, for it will drive them out or kill them."

Gout, French pox, pestilence, and "general pains" all are endangered by the taking of garlic, in the world according to Sauer. In a time when men in pain were willing to salve their swollen man-jewels with plasters, baked garlic (in hot ashes no less, which conjures remedies of a more Salem-like timbre), pepper, juniper berries, and boiled red wine combined to make a mean deterrent to obstructed urine. For the balled-up, as it were.

If anybody should have benefitted from garlic's medicinal powers, it was Darrell Merrell. Over a decade he'd eaten so much garlic that it perfumed him. He'd transfused his blood with a garlic-laced brew that could have boiled away any impurity. If garlic wards off vampyr, Darrell's breath could have slayed an entire countryside of undead.

No gout, no Vlad got him, but something cancerous in the gut. Not long after he stopped experimenting with heirloom garlics, shifting his attention instead to bouncing goats and banty chickens,

Merrell fell ill and never rose. Visitors who came to the farm for tomato plants in the autumn of his death wept at the news. I never spoke to Chester about it but I still imagine him weeping into his saucepan at the memory of the straw-hatted man of 365 garlics.

Darrell Merrell was founder and curator of the Garlic is Life symposium.

I love all the pastes and mashes that draw their spirit from garlic. My love for them can be traced in my blood and the proof they leave in my mouth. Things beyond pesto, though I need pesto like I need blood and air and bow at its altar each summer when the basil leaves thicken in the hot, near-dead earth. But one cannot live on pesto alone.

Catalonians make romesco, a sauce of nuts, pimentos, garlic and oil that is delicious with grill chicken and shrimp. In the chimichurri of Argentina and Uruguay, oregano overrides even garlic to make a heady dab for fire-cooked beef. In harrisa, the flaming condiment of Tunisia, dried red chiles are smoothed by oil and made spiritual by garlic. Garlic and olive oil are a marriage—always Lucy and Ricky, never Fred and Ethel—that every culture ordains.

Fergus Henderson, the pied piper of nose-to-tail cooking and eating, likes to ladle a bit of Green Sauce on just about anything, and his anything is more inclusive than yours and mine. In a recipe called "Green Sauce and Its Possibilities," he proclaims, "You have five wonderful things: capers, anchovies, extra-virgin olive oil, garlic and parsley. There is no end to the possibilities ..." Fergus slathers it on pig's ears, ox tongue and grilled skate.

His theory of aïoli is likewise swift and strong. He says introducing a recipe, "Aïoli often seems to be mistaken for a garlic mayonnaise, but this is not so. Aïoli is aïoli and eating it should be an emotional experience—it is strong, but that is its role in life." His version calls for twenty cloves of garlic to two and half cups of olive oil. Similarly, I have three recipes for Spanish mojo. All make one cup and all start with six cloves of garlic, peeled but left whole. They marry with sherry vinaigrette and red chiles to make mojo picon and colorado, and avocado to make mojo verde.

In our house, carrots are destined for the stockpot or the lunch bag, but here's a dish of carrots that can stand on its own:

Slice two of three of them diagonally, about half an inch. Strip the sleeves of a head of garlic cloves. Cover the bottom of a pan in olive oil and heat gently. Add the garlic and carrots and sauté until soft and golden. In the last minutes, add fresh thyme leaves and torn sage, to taste. Sprinkle with salt and serve.

Garlic is an old-world aromatic that my mother avoided out of fear and probably options, given her upbringing. None of her home-grown classics—fried chicken, salmon croquettes, chicken-fried steak, chicken and dumplings—contained it. Hence, I didn't dabble until I began making my own fettuccine al fredo and, later, my own pesto. There was precedent for this. Weaver concluded that "the Yankee kitchen rarely smelled of garlic unless it was to fumigate for disease." It is difficult for me to imagine a diet without garlic, but then a melting pot takes time to season.

At our hearth, we eat garlic more often than not, so it's difficult to isolate any favorite dishes—in fact, it might be easier to count those that don't rely on a least a clove or two—but if I had to pull a desert-island five, well ...

1. Poulet aux Quarante Gousses d'Ail—Chicken with 40 Cloves of Garlic. Forty.
2. A linguine dish from Danny Meyer's Union Square Café book that involves spinach wilted in olive oil flavored by red chile and 10 cloves of shaved garlic, then finished under the broiler with a healthy grating of Romano cheese and herbed breadcrumbs.
3. An Alsatian chicken sauté a la Jean-George Vongerichten of prunes, golden potatoes, bacon and whole, peeled cloves.
4. Gambas al Ajillo (shrimp pan-fried in olive oil, lemon, garlic, paprika and red chile, eaten with toasted baguette). Spanish bar food. Strand me now.
5. Oven-roasted potatoes garnished with chopped garlic and coarse sea salt.

If I were inclined toward a baked potato, I would take this noble cue from my beloved Fergus, who in theory could sue for my lack of license, which I indulge in only for you:

4 large jacket potatoes
20 cloves of garlic, peeled and left whole
enough duck fat to cover the garlic
sea salt and black pepper

Bake the potatoes in a medium oven until soft to the squeeze. Meanwhile, put the garlic cloves into an ovenproof dish and cover with the duck fat. Cover the dish and put into a gentle to medium oven. Cook until the garlic is totally squishy, then remove from the oven and whizz the garlic and enough of the duck fat in a food processor to give a very loose paste.

Let the potatoes cool enough to handle, then cut them in half lengthways. Scoop out the flesh into a bowl and add the garlic and duck fat paste. Stir thoroughly. When they have combined forces, season and return to the hollow potato skin. Pop into a hot oven until golden brown. Have you ever heard of such comforting fare?

You have now. "What a Baked Potato," from *Beyond Nose to Tail*, Fergus Henderson and Justin Piers Gellatly (2007, Bloomsbury). There, covered my bases.

Roasted garlic is transubstantial: a candied gem from a dynamite stick. One is Jekyll, one is Hyde. Ruth and Gehrig. One gruff and biting, the other soft and gracious.

In the raw, its juices never fully leave my fingers. Through my skin and affection, I have transmitted garlic to my next of kin. It is on their lips and ear lobes, in their hair and smudged into their bland, thin bellies. They eat it now without even realizing it. Unlike with onions, which are sweeter but also chunkier, a tomato sauce will hide a minced clove of garlic or three. Our two sons suck down the spaghetti strands and nod their heads, raise their fists and widen their approving eyes none the wiser.

The day after our first was born, I crossed the parking lot of the tree-lined mall across from the hospital to get his mother some food. The chimes that parade easily between such disparate Hollywood themes as *Love Story, Hill Street Blues* and *The Godfather* began to pipe The Carpenter's "Close to You." An aroma of garlic sautéing in the kitchen of P.F. Chang's scented the sickly sweet air. Any decent restaurant runs on garlic and spews its exhaust as proof. A restaurant that doesn't cook with garlic is to me a cathedral without ghosts.

I didn't have my own butcher until I was 40. We'd just bought a house nearby and I'd walk over any old time to get a piece of meat to grill. He followed the progress of our firstborn, then innocently lost track when we added a second. By then, the shop was working him hard. I saw him walking out the door one day, en route to his first vacation in eight years. Then, one day, he disappeared. He was cut out to be a butcher and, already, I miss him more than I've missed most tradesmen in my trading life. I look for him to surface, like the rich skin on a simmering stock. Where does a butcher disappear to, where does he go? What position requires such a skill set, save carving? Like the minister who married us but later switched to website design, does a butcher shift gears or simply move on? Surely there's an employer out there who can appreciate a man who knows how to sharpen a boning knife, doesn't mind a little blood on his pleats, comprehends the tender parts but embraces the hidden gems. Human resources, maybe.

CHAPTER XII

THE FAT OF THE LAND

C are for some bacon?" she asks, balancing a tray of tall, plastic cups in one hand and an empty bottle of wine in the other.

"Bacon ..." I say, like Homer Simpson might, and reach for a strip. It's a good quarter-inch thick, dried of its glisten and standing straight up as if starched. Like larded breadsticks. Between my fingers I feel the sandiness of the salt-sugar cure that has surfaced and sense the fat that's begun to soften. I cannot resist it and would love to see it in stores alongside Slim Jim or, better, in place of it. That said, I have no idea where I'm going to put it. Already I'm hauling a bar of lard soap and a bar of 68-percent cacao David chocolate studded with sea salt and embellished with pork cracklings. Also, a half-drunk bottle of Auteur pinot, a glass, a notebook, and a dozen-plus scorecards from the judges' table, mine among them.

In my belly, I digest the remnants of five prized pigs as tackled by five celebrity chefs, touring pros on a kind of circuit. They do wonders with loin, cheek, and untold lard while we in the gallery applaud, mingle and gorge. There is belly in my belly, fatback on my lips, and headcheese fogging my short-term memory. If not for the wine, my veins might well have congealed by now.

We are gathered on the campus of Oklahoma State University for a pork-and-wine taste-a-thon called Cochon 555, cochon being French for pig and the three 5s beings teams of cooks, vintners, and breeds of heritage hog. There is enough wine to drown a herd of swine, and a couple hundred guests to drink it. They're paying also for the privilege of seeing and eating what Old World pigs can become in the hands of creative cooks unbound by marketing convention and consumer behavior. For purposes of Cochon, there is no other white meat.

One of the chefs, Tulsa's Curt Herrmann, is smarting. In the middle of the $100 a head tasting, each cook and crew was required to plate and present their creations for the jury, sequestered in a side banquet across the hall. "It's bullshit," says Curt, a former personal chef to a descendent of William Randolph Hearst and no novice in the area of competition cooking. I feel for him, torn between loyalties as he is. But I feel more for myself and am too stuffed to do anything but chew the fat.

I still could taste the belly and refried beans Curt's Mexican sous chef brewed up, a joyously seasoned puree buoyed by lard. But it's the belly in my hand that somebody cured into bacon where I shift my attention. I observe it long enough to salivate and then I take a bite: It crunches magnificently, like a Heath bar. The balance of meat to fat is remarkably on the side of meat, for the strip is wine-dark, laced off-white with fat. I am too young, too unproven, to define the flavor, having grown up in the city eating the packaged strips that Oscar Mayer had stripped of all distinction. My mother's father slew and smoked hogs twenty yards from his kitchen door, but my mother tossed our salads with Bacos. I am staggering in the middle path, seeking the lost flavor of a long-ago truth on an unsure, unsung tongue.

Everywhere there are wine-stained glasses and nibbled bits of pork. There are lard-leavened strawberry shortcakes, pig's face terrine, blood pudding and "porksicles," which is a loin-and-lard pudding firm enough to cling to a stick. There is enough sausage—

sliced, encased, jellied, and puréed—to handle a White Sox double-header. Above it all there was the guest of honor, who entered the hall resplendent and dead, posing for pictures but incapable of basking in its star status.

Every gathering has a main event. Ours is a heritage hog—a thoroughbred of a Berkshire glowing Coppertone from the oven. It arrives on a white butcher block, gabled with bacon strips and gagged with a raspberry-red apple. It's a big pig, maybe six feet nose to tail, which for now remain attached. When it's brought into the room like some porcine Cleopatra on a cot, with ingots of baby Yukon golds scattered around her, a buzz and then a hush percolate into the rafters of the ConocoPhillips Alumni Center. Digital cameras begin to blink and wink at the art of it, lacquered for posterity in its own dripping fat. It can't be smiling but it is.

"Philippe!" shouts a cook wielding a very large knife. He means to summon Philippe Garmy, onetime Tulsa restaurateur and now professor in the culinary arts program at Oklahoma State University, long home to a proud program of hotel and restaurant management that's gone hand-in-glove with the college's agrarian past. Now, in the hands of Garmy, it seems poised to pluck from the other end of the food-and-wine plumage, the one training a slew of cooks and managers, hostesses and connoisseurs for positions in boutique spas, big chain hotels and kitchens versed in the language of local, seasonal and respectful food.

Now, in the hands of Garmy, the carver of the beast has placed a piece of snout. He holds it aloft slightly before sampling, then recedes into the mass of humans ogling what might as well be the last pig on the planet.

"Come on up folks!" the carver incites the crowd of pinot-drinking donors. "Get in there and go to town."

Applause breaks out in a rush. The faces in the crowd depict equal amounts of swagger and mock horror. A DJ cues Dwight Yoakam's cut of "Honky Tonk Man" and somebody feigns a two-step. Patrons tiptoe out of the crowd to pull greasy pieces of pig face off the table before making off with them like Cheshire cats. They stand and stare at the carving, at the carcass now compromised. They've been eating for a good hour and drinking wine for twice that, but somehow enough of them manage to muster another taste of pork to keep this portion of the evening from appearing more for show than tell. They appear happy, if in a frenzied way, the way their Cochon cohorts in Des Moines, Boston, San Fran, and elsewhere must also appear. It is early April, a succulent Spring, and nationwide Cochon is building up steam.

During a lull, I steal briskly to the table and snatch a piece of cheek. Back at my roost on the side of the stage, I tuck in: The outer membrane is impenetrable but the fat beneath it succumbs, slipping off my teeth and marinating my tongue. The fat of unspanked babes, of narwhals, of something Biblical and golden and newly calved.

The two Large women are seated near me, sipping wine but otherwise abstaining. Kala Large is the wife of Scott Large, of Thirst Wine Merchants, an Oklahoma City-Tulsa wine importer. Natalie Large is the wife of Chris Large, who for a while ran the Grand Vin wine shop in Tulsa. Kala stares expressionless at the feeding. Both women profess vegetarian leanings. Self-consciously, I suck at the fat that shines my fingers.

"I haven't eaten meat for 10 years," Natalie says, "but I appreciate the, you know ... ritual."

Ironically, maybe, it's the day before Easter. Men wear sportcoats over golf polos and women lift their cleaved chests in a salute to spring, their ankles delicately strapped. I sense that the officialdom of chef whites is the only thing keeping the festivities from going frat. Through the speakers, Dave Matthews' collegial thump sounds a preliminary note, a mating call for the conjugal and spontaneous alike. On my way out the door, I lift one last slice of head cheese.

Back at The Atherton, I pass up the elevator for the stairs in an attempt to pulse the pork and wine from my vessels. My gut is visibly rounded, achingly so, and I desperately seek the cool darkness of my quilted double bed. Lying there after a fitful shower, I flay myself wide across the comforter and listen to the workings of internal organs. The gastric juices bark and yelp as they sink their chemical teeth into a feast of utmost protein splendor. Against the flagon of wine, they fight for acidic dominance of my intestinal tract.

For an hour I submit, uncomfortably numb.

It's a thin crowd that rallies out on the patio after the last piece of pork has been eaten or tossed. Garmy's after-party has the makings of a kegger thrown on a school night and includes a few of the students from the culinary program, a lone kid playing pop standards on an acoustic guitar, and a couple of styles of Marshall Ale on tap. Ready to shift gears from pig and pinot noir, I grab a Old Pavilion pilsner and take a seat next to Garmy and a face I can't place.

Behind us, lights flood Old Central, the oldest building on campus. Built in 1894, it held all 144 of the college's students. By 1925, it had to be condemned when its sandstone foundation cracked under the weight of shifting Red Bed clay. The college had outgrown the one room by then anyway. A recent renovation restored Old Central mostly for symbolic purposes. New construction blossoms around it, adding to its aura.

Across the patio the muscular blond plays "Take It Easy" under a portico. The guy who looks familiar rocks his head in time. We sit quietly taking in the Frey-Henley melody, exchanging grins and glances at the well-known chords.

"Mark, do you know Stan Clark?" asks Philippe. Stan Clark, the owner of a burger bar turned T-shirt empire called Eskimo Joe's, sticks out his hand.

"Stan Clark."

"Yeah. Mark."

"Man, I love this guy!" Clark says, meaning the guitar slinger, who's apparently on loan from Joe's.

We trade early spring pleasantries of weather, wine, and song, since he seems happily engaged in the newest rock classic now a few notes old. I recall that Garth Brooks cut his teeth at a bar up the street, mixing classic and country rock with singer-songwriter ballads and honkytonk how-not-tos. Clark says, of the beefy blond, "He's my contribution to ... this."

Clark waves his hand to encompass the breadth of Cochon, now entering its sleepy Roman phase. Bodies sprawl about, some content and others lost. One guy slumps over a table, sleeping off too many glasses of red wine. For Cochon, all have given something. None more perhaps than its brainchild, Brady Lowe.

He drops down in the chair next to me, his brown blazer covering the majority of a white pig logo centered on his black T-shirt. Next to him plops one of the five chefs, a young hoss from Park City, Utah, who started in on the bourbon the moment the tasting ended. Under its influence, his eyelids hang like humidity. A fat cigar moistens in a corner of his mouth.

"Anybody driving to Oklahoma City?" Lowe asks. "We gotta get this guy on a plane by 6 a.m."

Nobody seems interested in going anywhere. Lowe leans back in his plastic chair and studies the smoldering end of his cigar. He rattles the ice in his bourbon. I tell him it feels more to me like a Scotch moment.

"No," he counters, "for me Scotch is a more contemplative drink. Scotch needs leather furniture and solitude. Bourbon ... it just goes." And to that he drinks.

Lowe is an odd sort of food revolutionary. Part small-school power forward, part indie bass player, he is more agent-executive producer than executive chef—the Scott Boras of the small-farm pig who treats his roster of clients like the potential boon they are. "Mark Newman is, to me, a rock star," Lowe will say in the quiet of the judging chambers, raising a glass to one of his Cochon jury.

Mark Newman is a clear anomaly, a pickup-driving pig farmer with a belly hanging over a belt buckle and Alice Waters' number in his cellphone. The Newmans invite high-profile chefs to their Missouri farm to interact with the livestock and see the farmer in action. "We bring 'em to the farm and let them carry the 5-gallon feed buckets. You've got to sell your story."

Part of his story involves bellies, would-be bacon that presented Newman with both a sickness and a cure.

"I was drowning in pork bellies, couldn't give 'em away," he said, prompted by a roasted cube of the the stuff sitting on the tines of his fork. "Then one day David Chang called."

Chang runs Momofuku Noodle Bar in New York's East Village, a far cry from Myrtle, Missouri. Momofuku ramen—a dish for which they beat down the door, and sometimes each other—is fortified by pork belly, pork shoulder, and a poached egg. For his talents and tendencies, Chang recently has made *Time* magazine's "most influential" list.

Newman once Fed-Xed a pig to Dallas for $892, and a loin to Tacoma that cost $80 bucks to process but $97 to ship. He supplies Armandino Butali's Seattle charcuterie, Salumi, whose guanciale (cured pig jowl) I cooked up for a pasta sauce one summer while in Seattle. Man, you think you know bacon. The cooks in this contest are working from three old breeds of pig:

Mangalitsa—A Hungarian breed two centuries old. Fatter than most. At the judges' table, I ate a piece of loin that was crowned by two-thirds back fat, like a bird's head with a gallon of plume. The Mangalitsa is a lard factory. Chris Shepherd of Houston's Catalan pureed a chunk of melted lard into a crouton-topping foam he called "mangywhip." He also made a lard soap that's still curing on my bathroom vanity.

Yorkshire-Hampshire—The farmer's cross they call it, they being English. Where the Mangalitsa relies on excess lard, the Yorky-Hampy combines the former's muscular stock with the latter's relatively high fat content. Early breeders in Kentucky called the imported Yorkshire "the thin rind." The legendary hams of Smithfield, Virginia, relied on Hampshire hogs. Yorkies are a mainstay of American feedlot production.

Berkshire—Three of the five chefs cooked with Berkshire, it being a kind of heritage breed harbinger. The Berkshire brings a lot of historical baggage: It was reputedly "discovered" by Oliver Cromwell, a man with a knack for uprooting purebreds of all walks. The Royals kept a Berkshire herd at Windsor Castle. The first hog documented by the American Berkshire Association (which founded the world's first Swine Registry on 25 August 1875) was a boar called Ace of Spades, bred by Queen Victoria.

There are other fascinating, near-forgotten breeds, too numerous to mention, and compelling in their number. Among them: Duroc, Gloucester Old Spots, Ossabaw, Lacombe, Red Wattle, Tamworth, Jinhua, Belgian Landrace, which sounds like dancing, British Lop, which sounds like leftovers. I could go on, for the peerage is deep with noble breedstock. You wouldn't recognize them, but you can still see and taste remnants of the line in the Wattles and Old Spots now coming of tender age.

"I see a movement back to the people who aren't exactly interested in the rat race of life," Newman says, with confidence in a voice that longs for more David Changs in the world. His role as Cochon supplier, speaker and culinary judge is a conflicting triptych that nobody seems to notice, save perhaps Lowe.

The Cochon web site pronounces its "2010 US Tour" with the searchlights of a Hollywood launch party. It's got the Facebook, Twitter and Flickr feeds of all hip and promising sites these days, and it counts down its tour dates like a culinary Coachella. A busy man, Lowe stopped updating his blog in February after the Atlanta cookoff.

I got tabbed for jury duty, I like to think, because Garmy and I go way back. But I was also features editor of the local daily up the road in Tulsa, and if anything needed press it was Cochon 555.

A week or so before Stillwater, we ran an advance of the event accompanied by a photo of Ryan Farr—of San Francisco's 4505 Meats, and house butcher for Cochon 555—dismembering a hog for the Napa event the last day of February. Farr blurs in the background of the photo, while front and center stares a pig's head, its ears spread like an angel's wings and a slight smirk below its snout. The head is flanked by the four cleaved hooves. All of the pig will go into the pot, as it were. That is at least one of the selling points of Cochon.

When I called Lowe the day after to tell him the phones were ringing off the hook, he sounded incredulous. What he terms without pause the "responsible sourcing of protein," our readers had deemed "sick," "gross," and "damned disgusting." I tried to address the gap in a column but ran out of room, time, and probably context. Who can explain the lost art and life of the family farm to a supermarket society that's used to buying pig in cellophane—cold and pale pink and boned for convenience, most of the fat nowhere to be found and no sign that an animal once was there. Even those inclined to be receptive to Lowe's message aren't likely to have the choice of a Berkshire belly suddenly materialize next to the John Morrell honey hams and commodity loins and chops.

"It's a passion of mine to find the real story of where things came from," Lowe told me, and I partook of his quest in Stillwater, where the challenges to an all-pig, head-to-tail feed seemed more amenable than in Boston or New York. Most of the venues supplied at least a portion of their pork—small-farm, obscure-breed stuff hand-picked by Lowe—but he also brings a trailer of Iowa hogs in tow to each town.

(This backup plan will backfire on Lowe in Portland, Oregon, four tour stops after Stillwater, when he and Eric Bechard, chef of Thistle in nearby McMinnville, beat the hell out of each other outside the Old Town strip club. At issue: the fact that Iowa, not Oregon, pigs took the trophy. With Brady Lowe and his traveling heritage breeds, there's seldom a lull in the proceedings.)

The night is youngish but I decide I've had all the consumption I can stand. Walking back to my hotel room, I choose a corridor that reeks of new and old academia. Down an arched walkway of compelling shadows, I traipse across bricks etched with the names of big donors to the alumni center. Halfway up the walk, through a lighted door, I see Garmy and Lowe and decide to stick my head in to say goodnight. Before I can open my mouth, Garmy points to a leather sofa. "Give me a minute," he says and I lay down on the cool cushions.

From my back I stare up at the wooden beams crossing the ceiling while Garmy and Lowe talk shop. They're at it long enough that I contemplate a nap, but then Lowe's gone and Philippe's recharged. "Marco! Get up ... we're going to eat Japanese."

A blonde pulls a car into the drive out front and a door pops open. I climb in back, leaving shotgun for Garmy. We leave the lights of campus and drive south toward what's left of downtown Stillwater. Hipsters hang out in the sidewalk in front of Louie's Grill & Bar, which seems like the only thing with a pulse still open. The hipsters huddle beneath the neon sign, smoking and toeing the pavement.

The blonde turns west at 10th Street and pulls up to a small building vaguely landscaped with shrubs and bamboo. It looks like we're going into a laundromat.

But inside Tokyo Pot, Garmy's army are in the final throes of controlled bacchanalia. Steel pots of Korean shabu shabu sit atop burners set into tables of slab concrete. Ceramic bowls of stock and uneaten vegetables litter the place, along with several dozen Sapporo empties. Barley and garlic smells permeate; pop music blares. The young proprietor, a wiry Asian named Dean Martin, attempts to plug the dyke.

"No more! No more! I cut you off!"

He commands the crowd with feeling but it's largely for show. They've taken over the Tokyo Pot and he has enough pride to put his foot down somewhere. His young apprentices rally around him and start clearing dishes. Friends and lovers lazily remove their elbows from tables and drain cans of near-dead lager, but nobody is in a hurry. Other than Dean.

Alex Kroblin is the young turk in charge of Thirst Wine Merchants' Oklahoma City operations. He's a fit, wiry type with a well of a constitution when it comes to drinking and talking wine. The life of any party I've ever seen him at, he's not about to let this one end. Kroblin slides his arm around Dean Martin and attempts to soften him with industry bullshit and genuine affection. They yell back and forth at each other, gesturing wildly like a couple of mountain stags locking horns. When they power hug, I feel it's safe and I go to the bar and order a Hoegaarden.

After things calm down, Alex introduces me to Martin, a 29-year-old go-getter who acts like he's running a place ten times the size. The Urban Spoon reviews of Tokyo Pot seldom omit him: "Dean, is super-cool." "Dean was awesome!" "Dean is great and is committed to showing every customer a fun and unique experience!!" With a pack of his underlings, hostesses, and kitchen crew smoking on the sidewalk steps, Dean sets out for me the master plan.

"It's no good here, I feel trapped! I take my act to Oklahoma City, to Tulsa." He says it like he has a chip on his shoulder, but Martin moves too fast for one to remain there long.

I tell him to stay put, that there's too much of everything in the cities: too many sushi spots and failing noodle bars, too much Asian buffet, too much asphalt parking space. He writes me off with a wave of his tiny, emphatic hand.

"Look around you," Dean says, spanning his fingers over sleepy 10th Street. "This is the ghetto, man!"

Back inside, I pick up a conversation that I'd begun hours earlier over something bacony with John Cooper, one third of a Stillwater band called the Red Dirt Rangers. Cooper likes wine as much if not more than he likes swine, and he presents something of a conundrum I feel in this neck of Oklahoma where Bud longnecks and Ford flatbeds reign supreme. Even without a microphone and an amp, Cooper strikes an inspirational chord.

We'd been discussing something we'd labeled the "Stillwater vortex." It can't have been a novel idea, but something about Dean Martin and his Tokyo Pot seasoned the theory even further. Amid bamboo curtains and acid-washed concrete floors, we start identifying vortices: Garth Brooks, of course; Boone Pickens, the thrillionaire raider with a fondness for building things, mainly stadiums; Stan Clark (an award-winning Australian rock band calls itself Eskimo Joe); the All-American Rejects, which sums up Stillwater in three words; and the whole Red Dirt genre, tangible enough to rally cross-country allegiances, spectral enough to blur boundaries.

Cooper and I agree, over an impromptu toast, that it's partly to do with what's left of the collegiate atmosphere, likely a result of the landscape—Stillwater, in the middle of nowhere, being possibly the center of several universes—and largely the influx of cash. It could be fortunate coincidence, but why leave it that on a night like tonight? So, on a pork-and-wine Easter eve, we shake on it. Then Cooper disappears, some rider on the storm of happy uncertainty, back to his roost in nearby Glencoe, I presume.

Dean really wants to close now but Alex, thirsty man of Thirst Merchants, has more in store. We pile into the car and follow him to Zannotti's, the only wine bar in Stillwater. Going on 1 a.m., the bar is closing for the night: chairs are stacked atop tables and a whiff of ammonia tinctures the musty air. Our party, now eight semi-strong, approaches the bar as if parched from the trail, as if none of the last six hours had happened. The bartender turns tail and heads to the back room. Waitresses lower their heads and shuffle furniture, anything to avoid eye contact.

"Jeremy?" Alex says, as a young man in charge approaches with that closing-time look in his eyes. Alex resembles Kevin Spacey in L.A. *Confidential*, with his close-cropped hair, strong jaw, big grin and yellow sportcoat. Hands held out in a sort of reproach, he really looks like him.

"Let me call him," Jeremy says, meaning his boss Gary Zannotti, the owner now likely sleeping in a quiet home somewhere far from Main Street. We mosey to one end of the bar and wait. Jeremy returns shortly. "He says you can stay if you agree to let us mop the floors."

"No mopping, Jeremy!" Alex snaps. He pulls out a credit card and orders five bottles of wine in quick succession, a serious medley of high-octane cabernets, syrahs, and pinots noir. The manager wags at the bone and starts trotting.

I've known Alex since he was 4 and I was 14. His mom would drop him off to play with my little brother. I'd catch glimpses of them as I'd slip Yes's *Close to the Edge* off the platter and, say, Genesis's *Trick of the Tail* on, a move I used to perform with the precision of a ginsu going over a duck. I went through much of the classic and prog-rock pantheon like that, without so much as fingerprinting an LP or tearing a sleeve. When I see Alex, in spite of his wine prowess and Spacey charm, I picture on the platter Kansas's *Leftoverture* and Pink Floyd's *Animals* in the on-deck circle.

At this hour, it's mostly Cochon judges and chef friends of Garmy. Alain Müller, executive chef at the César Ritz Hotel School in Le Bouveret, Switzerland, stands next to me at the bar. I want badly to speak to him in French but it's hopeless. I know enough to open the door but not enough to enter it. Instead, we scratch the surface on a few topics and sample myriad reds.

"Olivier," Alex says, holding up a bottle, "you ordered Heitz?"

Olivier Boudin, general manager of the Oklahoma City Golf and Country Club, confesses. "Nobody orders Heitz anymore!" he says, and it's true. The label, familiar at a glance, once had more caché. Looking at the bottle of Sineann in front of me, with its Celtic artwork and red-black contents, I could almost trace the new lines of dominance shifting in this budding millennium. Speaking that morning on campus at a pre-tasting panel discussion, Scott Shull of Raptor Ridge in the Willamette Valley called it "organizing industries."

"It's all about market segmentation," Shull said, "and navigating the river of how the population is changing."

It's 2 a.m. and I for one am glad the bar is closing. We drain our glasses and wipe our lips, now more tannic than fatty. On the curb out front, we say our goodbyes and split into cars. I am glad also that the blonde is driving, though I feel confident I could find my way to the hotel on foot, having spent my first semester here. But she won't let me, and it such a cool and lovely night with so much to walk off.

She pulls up in front of The Atherton and I climb out. Garmy and I shake hands and make future plans. This time up I take the elevator. In bed, I watch the moonlight until it invites me to sleep. The morning will come early, with me on the road by eight to make chapel. Easter Sunday and afterward as always pink ham in rind-free, maple-glazed, spiral-cut slices.

I found a stone on the beach at Samish in the San Juan Islands and pocketed it. It is hardly precious, but I ponder it often. On that same beach, we found Paul Blau's oyster beds. I'd never seen such sleeping beauties. Their meat was the perfect complement of mineral and brine, and quiveringly fresh. And big. One got caught in a throat, hanging half-in and half-out, like a second thought. Paul Blau pulled an oyster knife from out of nowhere and picked apart a pickled oyster in one pry. It was pure magic. "Here," he said, "you try." We took the knife back to the beach house with our oysters, two bags full. There, I broke my "no oysters and martinis" rule, and nothing more got broken.

CHAPTER XIII
OYSTERS

Mediterranean Oyster Symphony No. 3

She pitched her tables at the far end of the market, where the route N112 threatened the Café du Balcon on its way through Saint-Chinian. On the outside, she was a hard, old gal, with a raw pair of hands, shards for teeth, and a lace of black beard that grew close against a sharp chin. Inside, she was sweet. The voice that rang shrill in the market stalls fell, face to face, soft and patient.

She sold her oysters by the kilo, measuring the order with rusted scales. One kilo I ordered tipped the weight dead even, but then the *madame maritime* tossed another five fish onto the pile and bagged them in plastic. A kilo plus for two euros. In those days, less than two dollars.

I turned a corner and the Thursday market under the trees vanished in the rented rearview mirror. In several hours, we'd be on the other side of the world and far-removed from our sunny southern sea, as distant from oysters as a man can be. I took the curve to climb the hill and the oyster dame, and the salty scent that trailed her, was gone.

I once occupied myself with a dozen Cherrystones at the touristy Union Oyster House near Boston's Faneuil Hall. They were big as catcher's mitts and about as chewy. I ordered them because they were a few dollars less than the Blue Points, which I knew to be oysters. Cherrystones are not oysters; they are clams, and they chew exhaustively.

Since then, I've eaten oysters at enough corners of the globe—Boston and Wellfleet, Paris and New Orleans, Dublin City and Samish Bay—to whet a proper appetite. At Sete, a port town on the Mediterranean, they cultivate them on piles that protrude from the bay in even rows. At nearby Narbonne, they shuck them for you, and you carry the tray to the roughhewn café called Chez Jo and have the barmaid who smokes in stiletto pumps pour you a cold white wine, or two. A glass, in my experience, seems to last six oysters long. Oysters are bar food. The by-product of that is convenience; you eat while somebody else works.

"The sweet spot for shuckin' is at the back," said a shucker I know. "There's a little valve that's a bit weaker than the rest. I'd bet I could shuck a dozen in a minute and a half."

Historically, I snuck whole tins of smoked oysters from my mother's cupboard, letting them ride atop Ritz crackers—a dozen canapes straight out of a Betty Crocker cocktail spread. It was child's play, apparently, as I've not eaten them smoked since.

Each September, at Clarenbridge on Galway Bay, they fête the oyster with drafts of Guinness and, it's said, Black Velvet, though I'm not sure what passes for Champagne in west Ireland. At El Rio Verde, my local taqueria, I've made do with a half-dozen that bore the tepid, milky quality of the gulf oyster in summer. One spring at a local grill, we toasted—a dozen friends and I—my soon-to-be son with a feast of grits, potatoes, crispy onion rings, and rib chops. I, the sire, christened the ship with a dozen Quilcene Bay oysters, flown in from Washington State for the festivities. I paid accordingly—for them and the two martinis that preceded them. Lucas came in March, an R month[1] for what it's worth.

---

1 Warming water is the oyster's cue to spawn. Such an oyster, traditionally, was less of a specimen, being in a constantly spent state, and was likely to be challenged, both texturally and taste-wise. Hence, the belief that they are best eaten out of summer. Modern cultivaton techniques have all but eliminated such variability.

Mediterranean Oyster Symphony No. 1

The gift from our English landlady: a kilo of oysters de Thau. Denis, her 87-year-old hubby, had purchased them after a boat trip. The near-deaf Denis captained, and Margaret was his mate. They eloped up the Canal du Midi aboard his modest ship, sailing in off the Atlantic and settling in the south of France.

"You know they named a color for it," Denis told us, squinting up into the sky. "Yes. Mediterranean blue."

Maggie gave me her oyster knife, knowing it'd come in handy. Stubby little thing, snub-nosed and pointy, with a short, fat handle for stabbing and twisting. For assassinating bivalves.

"Take it, love," she told me. "And drink this with them."

A bottle of Picpoul de Pinet, the local white wine sold up and down the N112 from Montpellier to Marseillan, land of Noilly-Prat vermouth. My mouth began to spritz.

"Lemon?" I asked.

"Well … Let me tell you. We were on the boat last week and this old girl took the loveliest oysters and smothered them in shallots and vinegar. Well, I said to ma'self, Why would you go and do a thing like that? They're quite lovely just on their own, aren't they? Why ruin them?"

And with that, I took the kilo home and stood over the sink, wrestling the coarse rocks, alternating between slurps and sips. Somewhere in there, the oyster and the wine became one. I got pretty good with the knife, too, but I soiled an oven mitt in the process.

Oysters were in high season along the Mediterranean. Christmas was 'round the corner. Maggie'd bought herself an oyster chipper, an inventive little device that made the knife expendable. Rather than probe the hinge to pry open, you simply clipped the shell at the opposite, fragile end. The chipper opened a tidy enough hole through which to pry an oyster. Armies of starfish, on the other hand, attack oyster beds en masse, tearing at the shell[2] with their

---

2 Composed primarily of lime, the two halves of an oyster shell emerge within 24 hours of birth. They attach to most anything—a boot, a rock, a golf ball, another oyster—hence the varying shape. An oyster spins its shell, spider-like, building its history in layers, like the lifetime of hockey champions etched on Lord Stanley's Cup.

many tiny teeth until it breaches. The oyster drill, another creature aptly named, will bore a hole with its tongue and subsequently suck the meat free.

Me, I waded in head first, knife in one hand, wine glass in the other. Cracking the mystery of the oyster.

If freshness be the measure of any food, then, when it comes to eating seafood in landlocked places, oysters are a safer bet. Nothing else comes close, for all else is dead even before it lands, its eyes locked in a deep freeze, its flesh stiff as a board. How long dead it doesn't matter. The oyster, still living when you chomp it raw, has them beat. Thus, here in the land of man-made lakes, where not even the deepest wind carries on it a hint of the sea, I can arm-wrestle a fresh oyster and, as it lives, eat it to death.

Hence, an oyster wish: A dozen broad Belon, saving a dash of the liquor of one to dirty a martini, splashed with a dollop of Noilly-Prat and garnished with a pearl[3] onion. The liquor of the other eleven becomes a poaching liquid—for a Dover sole, gently braised until opaque, then to be crisped in brown butter. After that, we sail.

My mom's oyster stew—a milky broth in which too few tiny meats breached the slick of surface butter, and the oysters canned of course—lent just enough flavor to distract the butter and milk and pepper. I taste it still.

My Dad eats only fried oysters[4], but I don't believe one can eat

---

3 It's genus pteridae, by the way, not ostreidae that produces the pearl. (Pteridae is actually more of a mussel.) And it does so by spinning its fabric around an indigestible food particle, versus a grain of sand, which it will expel.

4 A good recipe, for those inclined to cook their oysters: You'll need some cream, spinach, bacon and oysters. And, for the oysters, some flour, two beaten eggs, salt and pepper. And olive oil. White wine, or vermouth in a pinch. First, tear several spinach leaves off their stems and blanch them; set aside. Then fry two strips of bacon in a little olive oil until crispy but not dry. Remove the bacon and drain on a plate lined with paper towels; crumble it up. Leave the fat in the pan and add enough olive oil to reach a quarter-inch or so up the sides. Heat it to medium. Pour some flour on a plate and season it very liberally with salt and pepper. Dip the oysters in the egg, then dredge in the flour, coating them well. Fry in the oil until golden brown on both sides. Remove, with the bacon, to a warm oven. Pour off the oil. Deglaze the pan with a splash or two of wine, enough to allow yourself time to scrape up the bits of flour stuck to the pan. (Wooden spoon!) When you have about a glaze, pour in some cream. (Four oysters needs about half cup of cream, eight about a cup.) Stir the cream into the glaze; there should be enough flour in the pan to facilitate a light roux. When the cream begins to thicken, add the blanched spinach leaves and heat through. Pour the sauce onto a plate (or two) and arrange four oysters in a cross. Garnish with bacon bits and serve.

only fried oysters and be called on oyster eater. When Anthony Bourdain called the oyster the perfect meal ("It comes with its own sauce!") he meant raw. But I love fried oysters as I love my father: I blindly favor them raw, to the point of forgetting how truly much I adore them fried.

The French tend to mistrust any oyster beyond raw. My copy of *Larousse* lists 33 preparations for them other than raw. Chicken, raw being not an option, gets some 300.

Sometimes, when an oyster glides across my tongue, I am reminded of a girl I kissed as a teen, her own moist tongue briny from a bag of sunflower seeds. A tongue is an oyster: silky, slippery, salty, labial, sublittoral.

"We begin with oysters. Not everyone does," quip the editors of *The Epicure's Companion*. 'Tis true. Half or so of all I know enjoy the bivalves, the others never. Where the oyster resides, there is no halfway house. My explanation for this, examined from within, is that oysters are not an acquired taste. The first oyster you eat, however young or cautious, will move you either to an lifetime of enjoyment or a revulsion from which you never recover.

When my in-laws brought a burlap sack of Gulf oysters up from Texas, we spread the table in a frenzy. And I swear, my timid sister-in-law endured a single oyster—her eyes swirled in a panic, and her mouth would not let go the gross of the meat, slick with the soup of the sea.

"It won't go down," she gargled.

"Swallow it!" said her sister, my wife.

She did. And two more after it, and they more elegantly. She's in. She's hooked! She may not eat another for ages—she'll never eat two dozen—but the day she does, by God, is her age of enlightenment.

I don't swallow. Well, ultimately. Others, I've heard, only swallow—they turn the shell up and slurp that sucker down, doing with the liquor for taste, I guess. It's not a heartless idea, an oyster's liquor being essentially its blood. Nonetheless, I chew the oyster, the same way I chew the grilled beef, rather than just tip the plate and drink the blood. In fact, I don't precisely chew on the oyster meat. Gently crush is more like it. It's almost a reflex: The teeth want to grind any meat. Of course, the oyster will not be ground; a couple of light chomps and gravity does the rest, the creature slicks his way down my gullet, where I assume acid makes short work of him.

Or her. Since the male and female share identical sexual parts, who can tell? Like it matters. You're not eating sex. Or are you? "Oysters are a food," writes Mark Kurlansky, "that loses charm when it becomes a staple."

According to Henry Mayhew's *London Labour and the London Poor*, in 1851, 500 million oysters were sold at Billingsgate Market. That's a 185 oysters per subject. Cheers.

Before the Tulsa Public Schools dropped oyster-eating as a fundraiser, the winning contestant slurped some 250 for a Main Street crowd of sandwich eaters. Gibbon wrote of a first-century Roman emperor, Vitellius, eating a thousand. Well, when in Rome. In New York, at say Balthazar, a Vitellian appetite today would run you $2000 easy. On Coney Island at the turn of the century, 1,000 oysters were a bargain at a dime apiece. The "Canal Street Plan" of the 1870s boulevard vendor was downright licentious. "All you can eat for six cents!" From 1883, *The Oyster Epicure*, a quote: "Something must be wrong with me! I have eaten 120 oysters and upon my word of honour, I don't think I am quite as hungry as when I began."

Such largesse was bound to have other consequences. By the 1950s, New York waters were off limits to oyster fishermen, thanks to overfishing and, later, pollution. Undeterred, cagey Staten Island old-timers would wait for the water temperature to drop to 40 degrees for four days or so, then fish oysters—in the belief that a non-feeding oyster (they go dormant at that temperature) would purge himself of everything in four days and be therefore fit enough to eat. Raw.

The 1970s saw an end to even that, when a stupid stew of chemicals—zinc, copper, chromium, lead, nickel, DDT, dieldrin, endrin, heptachlor, hydrocarbons, heavy metals, PCBs, asbestos, solvents, and even Agent Orange—found their way into New York Harbor. And the oyster was lost at sea.[5]

---

5 Oysters date to the Cambrian period, 520 million years old. Remarkably, they've changed little in the last 65 million, coming of age alongside man, their greatest enemy, natural or otherwise. Except, of course, when they disappear.

Mediterranean Oyster Symphony No. 2

We stood at the sea wall watching November push gray swells full of froth and sediment onto the boulders below. We looked and listened, recording the crash's echo for posterity. The Mediterranean, for us, had come to mean southern France, for sure, but also Spain's Costa Brava and Corsica's deepest blues, and myriad ancient ports[6] too numerous in even a year of idling. A time before the sea would become too distant even to fathom. We stared out at sea, watching gravity make waves.

Out at the end of the pier stood a flat shack. We entered for oysters and found them—chunks of black rocks steeping in sea water, set off by bags of sunny lemons. Bought two kilos for nothing, or next to it, and savored the bargain as if it were on the half-shell.

We drove them back to Saint-Chinian, up to Denis Haley's doorstep, returning the favor of a year prior, when similar samples arrived in a blonde box lined with a green matt. I recalled wrestling the little beasts then and envied Denis not a little for the battle that was to ensue. Even if it were to be waged by Maggie, brandishing her chipper.

In the end, I ate far fewer oysters the year of 2002 than I set out to. I've never eaten enough. I suspect I never will.

---

6 Like Greece. The doyens of the ancient city-states were known to vote by etching the inside of an oyster shell. Sometimes, the decision would be whether to banish, yea or nay, a citizen from the ranks of a village. Hence, our word ostracize.

Pulling up to a barbecue joint, I am nothing shy of a junkie. I enter and find a dark spot to sit. Hunger boils inside a neglected hollow. My eyes dart across the menu for deletions and surprise omissions. I worry whether I'll get the good stuff, or if it's being held for the sheriff's posse. Ghosts in overalls walk past, missing teeth and squinting. Guys in golf shirts shoot me queer looks. I eat fast and pay with cash. I get back in the car, wipe sweat from my brow and drive off in a daze. More often than not, there is a cop parked in the gravel lot.

CHAPTER XIV

BARBECUE TO THE RESCUE

East-Coaster Adam Perry Lang speaks of pork in terms of "delicate sweetness" and "lovely fat" before speaking geek. "Without getting too scientific," he begins and then pays homage to the realm of collagen, the gelatin-like membrane that slow-cooking renders without mercy. The slow heat loosens the collagen and the strands of protein succumb. "Pork is built for barbecue," Lang contends. His book, *Serious Barbecue*, takes a run at meat, pork especially, with swords flashing. Lang employs a series of baths, brines, bastes, glazes, mops, rubs, and finishes to take meat from raw to war.

Lang's famous for Daisy May's, a Manhattan barbecue spot, if such thing can be; for Carnevino, Mario Batali and Joe Bastianich's Vegas steakhouse, where he runs the meat locker, and where a one-pound New York strip costs $54; and Robert's Steakhouse in the Penthouse Executive Club, where filets can mean a number of things. Lang ducked out of Robert's in 2008.

"It was a great opportunity and fun project to develop," he told "Grub Street," the blog of *New York* magazine. "But I'm now focusing my attention on Daisy May's, Carnevino, and everything else beef-related."

Where's the beef? Montana, where Lang's own cattle ranch offers a steady supply. With barbecue on the books, beef looms on the horizon. To me, it sounds like a final, lone frontier.

B arbecue to you may mean beef, as in brisket. I have wolfed my allotment of smoke-black, pink-ringed brisket and I will again. But not if the same menu offers pulled pork or racks of ribs. Unless that menu is Cooper's in Llano, Texas, where the brisket is sold by the pound, served on paper and I'm told tops any mesquite-smoked meat ever eat. The sauce—a blend of ketchup, vinegar, black pepper, Tabasco, lard, and brisket drippings—smokes on the pit for two days. The briskets hit the pit for an intense smoldering, are then dipped into the sauce, wrapped in foil and finished over a low heat. Llano is west of Austin, in the heart of Texas Hill Country, a range of granite and mesquite fed by the springs of the Edwards Aquifer. The confluence of it all brings tears to my eyes.

I have driven way out of my way for barbecue, pulled by animal magnetism. In an era of half-hour lunches, I have driven into the sticks for two-hour barbecue sitdowns. It's culinary hooky and I consider it payback for enduring the hundred-degree summers and strip-mall geography of my native state.

Barbecue joints and funerals are generally why I wade into backwoods Oklahoma. The small towns of Ada and Vian, Pink and Maud, and vast others are where my people pass on, and where wood-filled ovens send up smoke signals. Barbecued meat is why I sidle up alongside the narrow-necked chainsmokers. Eating among these smoky souls, I long for absolution and absent friends.

When I hear of such a place, I chase it with a kid's Christmas eagerness, or a martyr's last stand. Indeed, what are barbecue joints but churches with wooden benches, passed plates, countless blessings, and unconfessed sins? I push away from these tables guilty as Caligula with the evidence of gluttony already growing bacterial between my teeth.

I went on a photo shoot with a coworker and for lunch we rolled south of the Arkansas River to a pit called Wild Horse Mountain Bar-B-Que. I'd heard tales of the crotchety old hoss that ran the joint on his terms, who picked his teeth with rib bones and swallowed links by the rope. "They don't even have running water," I'd hear.

We rolled in on a sunny, hot afternoon. All of Cherokee County seemed AWOL. White smoke rose from behind the place in thick, lazy wafts. Wild Horse sits at the foot of the hill from which it takes its name, like some last-chance saloon. Stapled to the counter are the business cards of every redneck lawyer inside the county line.

"Who's that?" the photographer asked, pointing to a fuzzy photo off-center in a faux-wood frame.

The old boy said, "That's Johnny Paycheck's band."

"Where's Johnny Paycheck?"

"Probably on the bus."

In the dingy black-and-white, a couple of the boys are wearing wife beaters and all of them sport Hank Thompson straw hats and Don Felder beards. Styrofoam cups hide whatever they were drinking.

In spite of the reviews, I can't rave about the Wild Horse pork ribs. For one, they weren't ribs. More like smoked loin with the rib bones frenched as if for a city menu.

"Whoa," I said to the old boy. "That's like the whole loin."

"I like meat on my ribs," he said, his mouth torn between a smile and an indictment.

We paid the check, paid one more homage to Paycheck, and left Wild Horse Mountain probably for good.

Over the hill and around the bend, on the banks of the now-navigable Arkansas, Bryant "Big Country" Reeves—the pride of Gans and onetime Vancouver Grizzly—has built a house and a prefab gym for pickup games. Something tells me that Country, in the day, packed away a smoked pig or two.

Late last spring, not long after Jack and Diane called it quits, Jack picked me up in his beat-to-hell Volvo and drove me to small-town Sperry for a picnic at a place called Buffalo's.

He was all pumped up about a recent Tulsa Tough bicycle race that had lured Floyd Landis to town. We talked about that and Chicago baseball and the call of the wild Jack is wont to heed often enough to call it a vocation. Jack drove through the rich green pasturage east of Sperry, past the tag agency and the United Pentecostal church, curving north into the bedroom community that could have been.

"Haulin' Pork Butt Across America" proclaims the logo of Buffalo's, depicting a raging Bulwinkle-esque bison pushing a pink pig in a wheelbarrow. When you click on the "BBQ Restaurant" link, a picture of Donny Teel's rolling pork shop appears with its built-in smoker and roll-up windows. When in town, Teel opens for business in the gravel lot of a Daylight Donut shop. The world's largest Daylight, I am told, is in Bucharest, Romania, where in addition to donuts you can drink a beer and eat a sausage. You can also smoke to your heart's discontent.

Donny Teel exhibits all the credentials of a barbecue master. In fact, he's Exhibit A: He sports the hair of Bruce Jenner and the beard of Bruce Dern. He's got sad eyes that droop out from under a hickoried brow. He's a man of few words who'd rather let his ribs do the talking. His belly could be holding a sea turtle. He is perhaps the best pitmaster in three states.

"It's on me," Jack said, ordering one combo dinner that he claimed would satisfy us. "Nobody ever thinks there's going to be enough, but there always is."

We sat on the bench of a wooden picnic table, eating and talking, while traffic took the turn into town proper. Indeed, it was the perfect amount. Not an exploding-belly amount, but a properly satiating kind. We didn't talk about Diane, like we didn't one other time I was supposed to, when Jack came over for some steak and ale and explanation. Instead, we just talked and ate. Teel's pulled pork renders in the mouth with a velvet touch, and his rib meat falls from the bone at a mere glance. I said a man could eat this every day, he could. "We'll do it again," Jack said, fat greasing his lower lip. "Soon."

Soon. Right now, Jack's in Oakland helping his aunt and uncle restore sail boats. He likes to take a boat out in the bay and navigate it through the currents beneath Golden Gate, mindful of the shipping lanes, the flotsam, and his limited prowess. On his way out west, he sent me photos of Sequoia National and Monument Valley, out past where the buffalo roam, out beyond the past life.

There is the Billy Sims who ran roughshod over the Big 8 conference during the last days of disco, and then there is Billy the barbecue champ. The former ran like Pheidippides and had the finest afro ever tucked beneath a football helmet. The latter wears Wranglers, starched white shirts, and a gold belt buckle big as a Frisbee. He's thicker through the middle, of course, and thinner on top, enough to make you hurt if you're old enough to remember when.

My dad ran into Billy Sims as he was in the process of opening up his first barbecue joint, Billy Sims Barbecue, in the Farm Shopping Center. Mom and Dad had been to Furr's Cafeteria—another of my father's institutions—and he made her drive by Billy's joint to check on progress. When they encountered Sims in the parking lot talking on a cell phone, my dad rolled down the window.

My dad's idols, in this very particular order, are Barry Switzer, Vito Corleone, Mickey Mantle, Billy Sims, and Billy Graham. Graham arguably could move up that list and probably will over time. But nobody touches the great Switzer, the Prince of Crossett, the Norman King. Sims, a soldier of Switzer's, is to my dad a holy relic—the onetime Son of Ran under Barry the Great. My dad's favorite films of all time are *The Godfather*, *The Godfather Part II* and a home video called *Oklahoma Football Legends Reunion*, a sort of roundtable bull session led by Switzer and attended by a legion of his prize recruits.

"Just imagine 33 of your favorite Oklahoma Sooner legends—all in one room at the same time," reads the Amazon review.

My dad leaned out the window to ask Billy Sims how the shop was coming. Before long, he'd wandered off into the endzone of nostalgia that's always capped with the story of how Switzer visited my dad's dad on his death bed. That's something I'll never forget, he always says.

"Hold on," Sims said, and started poking his phone. "Coach? Yeah, got a guy here wants to talk to you." Billy hands the phone to my dad who repeats the story. Remember, Coach?

"I do. Out on Northwest Expressway. You bet I do."

Cleaning out my parents' garage the other day, we came upon a too-large photo for the frame, a 4-by-5 enlarged to fit a 12-by-15. My dad's dad, Lloyd Kenneth Brown Sr., is wearing baby blue pajamas. An oxygen tube curls from his nose onto the lapel. Barry's got on a tweed sportcoat, blue button-down and a tie with mallards on it. Sims had graduated three years prior and the program was in tatters.

Barry and Lloyd gripped and grinned for the Kodak moment, the Sooners went on that weekend to rout Colorado 82-42 and my grandpa just went on.

"It's not just barbecue ... it's Boomer-Q!" Billy Sims attests atop his Web site, where the call for franchisees is loud and clear. Two-day shipping nationwide, for the Sooner Nation knows no geographic bounds, even if ribs don't travel as well as Saturday heroics. The "Half Back" is a half-rack rib dinner that sells for $11.99. A "Full Back" is full rack for $19.99.

There used to be an Ozark Mountain Smokehouse in the space that is now Billy Sims Barbecue, but it was all pre-cooked and cured in Fayetteville. Now, the smell of hickory settles over the Farm like it must have in the almost-unimaginable days before pigskins were punted. I like to think of it as payback for 1978, when the Razorbacks humbled the Sooners 31-6 and tarnished the bronze on Billy's brand-new Heisman.

We buried my young cousin on the hill in Okmulgee, home of hearsay, if not legendary, barbecue. An October, of all times, with Oklahoma crawling out from beneath another of its white-heat summers.

She was laid to rest and we in our train of cars and clothes migrated to the First Baptist Church gymnasium where lunch was being served ahead of a memorial service. We ate ribs and brisket beneath basketball goals, on folding tables draped in white. We ate, washed it down with tea and lemonade and soda, awaiting the exchange of songs, sad glances and exodus.

"Myrna buys her pies at Colemans," my mother said, Myrna

being my aunt, Colemans being another Okmulgee mainstay, and my mother's near non sequitur drifting up toward the rafters. I, on the other hand, was wondering where she bought her barbecue.

Fall is a good time to lay into a plate of barbecue. There is no digestible reason for this, it just is. The wood smoke that blends with whatever else happens to be burning across the plain and gets caught in the wind. I associate barbecue with the rustling of leaves and the anticipation of autumn rains. I have a soft spot in my heart for barbecue served in hard times.

Anyway, I was tonguing meat from my teeth as the pipe organ began its march, followed by singing and the bobbing of my aunt's head from neither joy nor tribulation but both. At the front of the altar stood an enlarged photo of my cousin, a great barbecue eater looming larger than ever.

I have been to the mountain top but the Promised Land eluded me: Closed on Sunday.

"Why visit Graceland when you can spend your time in this legendary back-alley dining room, gnawing flame-charred baby-back ribs crusted with the spice mix that made Memphis famous?" said *Esquire* magazine in July 1999 of the legendary Charlie Vergos Rendezvous dry-rub pork ribs. Then, three years later, they sent Tom Junod to say it better: "I ate like a king in Memphis, which is to say that I ate like the King, which is to say that I ate like a pig, which is to say that I ate a lot of pig."

Junod called the ribs of Rendezvous "fragrant."

Operation Torch hit Morocco and Algeria on 8 November 1942, laying the groundwork for an Allied assault of North Africa. The largest of the operations within the operation, Operation Brushwood, dumped 19,000 Anglo-American forces on the beach at Fedala. The weather got ugly and several of the boats, instead of landing, pitched and dove all over the port of Casablanca. Grant Hastings, inventor of the legendary Hasty-Bake Charcoal Oven, got his feet wet at Fedala. He witnessed his first SNAFU[1], with

1 "A SNAFU is military parlance for, "Situation normal: All fucked up." Debatably, it surfaced during World War II to descibe business as usual, however mangled. (Note the colon: It makes all the difference.) Though on the same side of the pitch, the Brits claim they, not the Yanks, coined the term.

landing boats tossing like autumn leaves. Patton landed at o8 hundred and the city was secured shortly thereafter.

When the smoke cleared, Grant ducked behind a cork tree to take a leak. From the other side of the tree, an old woman came running at him with a live turkey. After the fright, he negotiated a price and hauled the turkey back to camp. He plucked and dressed it, dug a hole in the sand and filled it with cork wood. He then took turns with a buddy, Louis Ciolino, turning the turkey over the coals on a stick. "Cork is a hardwood," Grant wrote, "so we slow-smoked that bird for hours."

To hear him tell it, this was where he got the idea for his Hasty-Bake—a tiny seed that fruited in wartime to blossom a few years later over beer, ribs and small talk. Grant was living in a bungalow by the river then, going into the backyard in the evenings, shooting the shit with future partner Gus Baker and dreaming of a mouthwatering metier. "It was there, in those sometimes endless hours, that I found my inspiration."

Grant Hastings, at least when it came to cooking, was not a man of secrets. He seasoned his steaks simply and grilled them with a van Gogh touch. He applied the right amount of smoke to his ribs, attentive to the sublime in aroma, color and texture. He pulled spices from his pantry one jar at a time. Cooking over fire, he was subtle with a capital T. *Popular Mechanics* magazine called his invention "civilized."

"It wouldn't be an overstatement to say that I've dedicated my entire life to developing a machine that would, in my opinion, produce the best ribs a man could eat." He did, and it can, in the right hands.

They buried Grant in a neck of the woods called Floral Haven four summers after we'd met. Maybe a hundred witnesses were in attendance. I somehow expected more, whole legions of followers reeking of smoke and spice. The Presbyterian minister went through his paces, acknowledging Grant's impact in broad strokes.

Nowhere were the titans of outdoor cookery, the ones Grant tormented in dubious battle through the post-war rise and shine of American grilling. Where was George Stephen, king of the Weber Kettle, now that we needed him, and where Wade Busby, marketing force behind the Big Boy, who owned California the way Trump owned New York? When you die an old man, few survive to do the tale any justice. I departed with Tony Bennett's rendition of "The Best Is Yet to Come" hanging in the air like the reek of hickory smoke.

As odd as it is to pray for barbecue, I pray that there is fire in heaven and that it's being tended by Earl Grant Hastings Jr., he of the angelic touch who by then was ideally chilling beer on soft banks of icy clouds and preparing a benevolent rack of seasoned ribs for a slow baptism on the pearly grates.

I first drank them vicariously through Lt. Frederic Henry, the World War I ambulance driver of *A Farewell to Arms* whose love dies in a hospital on Italy's Great Lake, their "skinned rabbit" of a son tossed stillborn into a bucket. Early in the novel, Henry dives into a river to escape execution and, of course, ends up at the Paris Ritz. He descends upon the bar and socks away a few sandwiches and more than a few martinis. Having read up, I now take them on my own, one every few days and always with gin. I tend toward Gordon's, as did the Queen Mum until she entered Avalon. Juniper, a critical component of the spirit, contains elements of thujone, the chemical scapegoat that set absinthe back all those years. Thujone appears again in vermouth, so in a martini one gets a double-dip. I remember this whenever I go over the line with gin and it rearranges the alphabet in my mouth, even as I speak it. Gin tastes to me of a marriage: between an Icelandic madwoman and a Canary Islands alchemist. There is an Artic mist in her hair, a whiff of ling cod on her hands and ice in her veins. His beard is redolent of wood smoke and flecked with root stems, seeds and berries. A shaken, bruised and strained coupling—a convergence of improbables.

CHAPTER XV

IN THE COMPANY OF GIN

B arnaby Conrad III pointed out the home of the Mai Tai, its entrance obscured by palm fronds and banana trees.

"That's the old Trader Vic's room," he said, handing his keys to a parking attendant. "It's now a pretty popular Vietnamese restaurant."

Le Colonial, it's called, and it manages to fit. When it was Trader Vic's, the area known as Cosmo Place, between Downtown and Little Saigon, was a nightlife destination. According to a website that tracks tiki culture, Queen Elizabeth II experienced her first-ever anywhere restaurant meal at Vic's in 1983, as a guest of the Reagans, no less. She drank a Tanqueray martini. That Vic's closed in the early '90s.

We walked up Taylor Street to the Bohemian Club. It was Thursday—bohemians' night out. Before dinner, we drank a No. 209 martini at an oak bar long and polished enough to have 10 pins at the end of it, surrounded by large oil paintings and the soft roar of men not at work. I stole a couple of paper napkins off the bar, the club's owl logo teetering across them.

I'd spied the No. 209 tucked among the other gins. It's a newish brand, produced locally in a distillery down at Pier 50, very near the spot where Barry Bonds Jr. used to plunk homeruns into the bay. A couple of sips in, I spotted the bottle next to it: Junipero, a small-batch offering from the folks who also brewed Anchor Steam, another San Francisco product.

"Hmm," I said. "Maybe we ordered in haste."

"I know Fritz," Barnaby said, referring to Fritz Maytag, who'd resurrected the old Anchor brewery and then sold it after an award-winning run. "He's 75 and in great shape. Beefy, not obese, you know? Like he could have played quarterback at Cal-Berkeley back in the day."

He suggested a trip up the coast to meet Maytag, but I suggested we drink a Junipero instead, as an after-dinner nightcap. The club ranks were beginning to thin and last orders were being taken. I wondered if anybody would awaken the older gent I saw napping earlier in the library, his body sunk into the puffy, tan leather of a club chair. I thought of him being left there, like Corduroy, to be discovered in the wee hours by a security guard making rounds.

"Next time," I said about Fritz, sipping the Junipero and making a mental tasting note I soon forgot.

"Anyway," Barnaby said, chinking glasses, "welcome to San Francisco."

H e'd grown up here, in the shadow of his writer and saloon-keeper father, drinking ginger ale at one end of the bar while the likes of Tyrone Power and Ava Gardner drank gin at the other. Dad Conrad named his bar El Matador, after a novel he wrote on bullfighting called *Matador* became a surprise bestseller. He chronicled those days of wine and roses in a delicious tell-all, *Name Dropping: Tales From My Barbary Coast Saloon.* (A dozen years before, though, he'd published a memoir of a different sort—*Time Is All We Have: Four Weeks at the Betty Ford Center.*)

With writers and drinkers, the olive often doesn't fall far from the tree. Conrad III followed in his father's footsteps with a fistful of books. One of them, *The Martini*, published in 1995, caught the front end of the wave that stranded 'tini menus across American bartops, recipe books in the stacks at Borders, and faux-vintage cocktail shakers on the shelves of Pottery Barn. It was my martini manifesto, a reference guide and devotional in ice-cold words and pictures. Its cover—a tightly cropped photo of a martini glass, its bowl glistening with the droplets of mid-chill—was the model of perfection I pictured when shaking at home during what historian Bernard DeVoto called, and Conrad quoted, "the violet hour."

The same year he published *The Martini*, Conrad met Maurice Kanbar, who couldn't drink more than two martinis without getting a headache. (Conrad's own theory, from page 120: "Even if there's no driving to be done, two's a pretty good limit.") Having the wherewithal and now the need, Kanbar invented SKYY, the quadruple-distilled, blue-bottled beauty that overran the vodka market in the 1990s, in large part because of that cobalt bottle, which he had to get produced outside the country because, he explained, "making glass is a dirty business. You have to have smoke and glass and ovens. Americans don't want to do that. They want to sit at a computer."

But the SKYY wasn't the limit. With his non-compete clause expired—he'd sold SKKY off to spirit conglomerate Campari in 2001—Kanbar now peddles Blue Angel (in a clear bottle of brushed glass), another ultra-distilled spirit in a market he helped saturate.

Kanbar's inventiveness manifests itself in all manner of productions—*Hoodwinked!*, the animated hit film; an 85-cent pair of eyeglasses he wants to distribute pro bono in third-world nations; *Hoodwinked Too! Hood vs. Evil*; Zip Notes, in which he put the adhesive in the middle so the paper wouldn't curl—but, in 2005, it ran to a few square blocks of downtown Tulsa. Kanbar now owns 16 buildings worth of it.

Always a bookish sort, Kanbar's properties have included, almost since its inception, Council Oak Books, the Tulsa publishing house struggling to make it in the world of Kindles and downloads.

(The firm has since relocated to San Francisco.) With Conrad, he'd launched a new imprint on Council Oak, Kanbar & Conrad, though he couldn't remember when or how he met his new partner.

"San Francisco is basically a small town and he's a writer. I like writers. If Barnaby Conrad is a writer, then I immediately have a compatibility with the man. Writers are my guys."

Mine too, especially when they fall in with guys who buy up downtowns in their spare time. You know, when they're not distilling spirits and publishing books. I'd been looking for a reason to get back to San Francisco. Now I had a couple.

"You know he was a tumler?" said one-time San Fransisco columnist Bruce Bellingham.

I pictured Maurice in circus tights, floating beneath the big top. I wouldn't put it past him. I shook my head.

"Not a tumler," he said, reaching for something to write on and finding it in his breast pocket in the form of a sealed envelope. "It's one of my many medical bills. I had a heart attack in June 2010 and now I have $94,000 in medical bills. And there goes one of them."

Bellingham took another sip of wine, scribbled something on the envelope, then handed it to me.

"A tumler, for you Gentile boys, is a man who's hired in the Catskill Mountains to break up the party before an opening act. So, he's really like a clown. Like Jerry Lewis. It'd be like me going from table to table, 'Hi, ya, how ya doin'!' It's a Yiddish term for a troublemaker. Someone who stirs it up."

Barnaby took a sip of his Blue Angel martini—a gin man seguing into vodka out of homage, I assumed, given that we were in Perry's on Union Street, Maurice's favorite spot, and he was to have been here with us. Kanbar calls a Blue Angel martini a "BAM," believing that a drink without a name is a bottomless well. ("The key to the business is a call," he said. "Like a Cosmo.") Barnaby downed his in an effigy-like salute to its absent inventor, while I paced myself with a Sierra Nevada.

"He wasn't a kid—maybe 19 or 20—and he's been a tumler ever since," said Bellingham. "But, he's cultivated tumling into a finesse.

Of course, no one around here knows what a tumler is."

Bellingham wrote columns for the *San Francisco Examiner*, and with San Francisco newspaper icon Herb Caen.

"I wrote jokes for him. I'd send him jokes everyday by fax. Puns, political metaphors. I sat in Herb Caen's office while he was ill and went through 59 years of his column, all gathered in leather-bound books. The *Chronicle* owns them. I thought, 'Where am I going to begin?'

"They had so much fun. You and I cannot imagine. Barnaby can tell you."

Caen and Conrad Junior inhabited a time in San Francisco when the word saloon was a term of endearment. When books were books and men were men and martinis were gin. You can still get a drink there, but the way the old boys—and their sons—tell it, things have all but dried up.

"Single women with dogs and fast-food restaurants and nothing else," Barnaby says of the future city by the bay.

Writer Rebecca Solnit, in her *Infinite City: A San Francisco Atlas*, plots 21 bars on a map of the city's legendary "6 a.m." saloons, so named for the hours they kept in order to better serve the dock workers leaving the graveyard shift. Service and software have replaced shipping, but the bars remain.

Beyond the living proof, there are the dead. Novelist Jack London had a San Francisco saloon mix vast quantities of martinis and ship them to his getaway in Sonoma. "Professor" Jerry Thomas, hands-on author of *The Bar-tender's Guide*—an 1862 classic that predates them all—made his mark at the Occidental Hotel on Montgomery Street. Thomas makes a good case (particularly for one deceased) for inventing the martini, or at least being its missing link.

Bellingham was in purgatory when Kanbar bailed him out. A local charitable house received a big gift for taking care of Bruce between gigs, courtesy of the man with the golden arm.

"I've not been upset with one gift that I've ever given," Kanbar told me. "But if you asked me about business deals, oh God, have I met snakes."

We left Bruce and Perry's for Bix, next stop on the "martini safari" I'd been promised and was doing my best to make a good show of. We drove up Laguna, jumped over to Broadway, and headed downtown.

Gold Street hides between Sansome and Montgomery, a few blocks in from the Embarcadero. It was called Gold Alley back in the day, when the burlesque clubs and watering holes of nearby Broadway teemed with all that was then rustic and possible about San Francisco. When Streisand was playing the Purple Onion before she was Streisand, and newsmen like Caen had the equivalent of 10,000 Facebook friends, all of it earned in the saloons and restaurants and nightclubs within earshot of here. Gold Alley is around the block from City Lights Bookstore on the diagonal at Columbus. Chinatown is near, as is American Zoetrope, Francis Ford Coppola's headquarters, where the ground-floor café proffers Coppola's own wines at a relative steal, and tempting plates of radicchio Treviso, spaghetti carbonara, and pizza *quattro formaggi*.

"This is Gold Alley," Barnaby said, pulling into a lane too tight to turn around in, and promising to tell me later about the time he shot a .44 out into the bay standing right here. I looked up over a warehouse roof to see the white apex of the TransAmerica Pyramid. That, the neon of Bix, and the headlights of the sedan were the only lights glowing.

We crowded around the bar at Bix, a restaurant I'd known only from an image in *The Martini*—of other people crowding around the bar at Bix. In the book, author Conrad, proprietor Doug "Bix" Biederbeck, painter Mark Stock, art dealer Martin Muller, Herb Caen, and others smile over a caption labeled "Neo-Martini Culture in San Francisco." In the foreground sits a very large bowl of crushed ice sprouting chilled cocktail glasses like so many spring crocuses.

Biederbeck likes his martinis cold, versus large, and to that end he serves them in small, tulip-shaped glasses, the gin cold enough to induce shock. "Here," he said, retrieving my cocktail from the bartender. "Drink that and I'll get you another."

I sipped, squinting at the peal of competing conversations, and a piece of the city's still-strong drinking culture revealed itself to me. Towering shelves of spirits glistened from the backlit bar. Fit, robust men in white jackets shook and poured in a dizzying blur of glass and ice and steel. A table ordered a lot of wine and the musty smell of Argentine Malbec forced its two scents—strawberry and spice— on an air already perfumed with heavier tincture. Older, moneyed-looking women brushed skirt hems with young, honey-eyed vixens while their collective men pushed empty glasses back for refills.

"You about ready for another?" Biederbeck asks me. "No, wait … Let's have a punch!"

He'd recently found Amer Picon through a London purveyor and pounced on a case. Its orange essence and dry bitterness begged for a punch, the definition of which varies, even among liquid historians. Two non-wavering components tend to be the presence of fruit, and the mixing of batches versus glasses at a time. (Esquire drinks writer David Wondrich outlined all the tasty possibilities in his 2010 book, *Punch: The Delights (and Dangers) of the Flowing Bowl*.) "When the case showed up," Biederbeck said, "there were only 11 bottles in it. My tariff, I guess. Here …"

He handed me a glass of punch and I turned to watch the band, all ivory pings and bracing snares and throat. The bigshots of old-school jazz play here, not that I'd know them by sight or sound. But Biederbeck, true to the name, is a student of both jazz and the drinks that tend to mingle in its presence.

Over the piano, singing a tune of its own, is a painting from Mark Stock's "The Butler's in Love" series. It's the first thing you see when you enter Bix and the last thing you take in before you pass the velvet curtain on your way out. It dominates the space the way the Eiffel does Paris, no matter the vantage point.

In "The Butler's in Love–Absinthe," the butler—a barely veiled Stock—leans into a jade-green wall, gazes at the lipstick staining an empty absinthe tumbler, and resigns himself to a life of subjugation and unrequited love. He hangs with his back to the crowd, which likewise pays him little heed.

Between Picon punches, Barnaby showed back up from somewhere down the busy bar. I'd been trading John McEnroe stories with a tennis fan named Renee Richards (not the U.S. Open Doubles finalist of sex-change fame)—she knew him in high school, I peed next to him in a New York theater. Anyway, I'd lost track of him. Barnaby, that is.

"Here," he said, handing me yet another punch, "I got you another drink. We should probably eat something. I realized I hadn't eaten anything all day except a piece of lemon meringue pie for lunch."

I stood two-fisted with my back against a marble pillar that stretched to the second-floor ceiling. A single window in a whole ceiling of them was opened to the late-January night. Oh, to be a bat in that belfry. Caen is dead, and Biederbeck a little thicker through the middle, but Bix is about as much like a photograph in a favorite book as a place can be, meaning every bit as good as you prayed it would be lest you feel your faith wavering. Of course, it could have been the cocktails. It always can.

Earlier, I'd asked Barnaby where Team Martini held court before the days of Bix. It was Alfred's.

Forgotten, but not gone—having moved from its original location over the Broadway Tunnel to Merchant Street, in the shadow of the Pyramid—Alfred's is a steak joint in the pre-Fleming's sense, meaning ripe, aged cuts smoked over mesquite and big martinis and Manhattans cold and keep-'em-coming. Kerouac ate there (and knowing him, drank) and wrote about it in *The Subterraneans*. Among old souls, Alfred's was the nostalgic choice in an environment of New Age imbibing.

"Everybody was drinking white wine and then going to the bathroom to do cocaine," Conrad said. "Well, we didn't want that. We wanted to do our thing out in the open."

There was a time when Barnaby Conrad III was among San Francisco's most notorious bachelors, eligible and elusive at once, as likely to be in his attic painting, or at the bar drinking, as he was being seen on somebody's arm. (A lot of that time is in an unpublished book titled *The Bachelor's Progress*, which his editor called "a sort of Tom Jones romp.") But then he married Martha Sutherland, an authority on contemporary Chinese art and a CIA operative of 18 years—two passions that must have played out strikingly when she found herself in the midst of Tianmanmen Square in 1989. But then she married Barnaby Conrad.

Of the lumber Sutherlands, she is, whose TV ads once employed country comic Jerry Clower in all his big-bellied bluster. Playing the Kevin Bacon game, that put Clower and Conrad at too close a remove for my comfort and taste. Yes, I had done the fanboy thing and chased my favorite writer (on ice-cold gin drinking and absinthe's "green fairy" wings, anyway) all the way to the top of Pacific Heights, sometimes called "Specific Whites" for the exclusive group that dwells there.

I'd chased him to a watering hole in a book where writers and drinkers mixed like vermouth and gin (or more likely vodka) in my mind. Yes, I was ashamed. But I was also on assignment.

"San Francisco is a drinking town," Conrad said, balancing a glass of Amer Picon as he might a combustive nitrate or some tonic of eternal youth.

I drank to that.

She lifted the fork to her lips and the metal caught a glint of sun for less than a second. She ate delicately, unaware of my stare. Torn bits of egg white clung to the tips of the tines, held there by runny yolk so very gold. Over the witch's ruby red lips the bite went, but before it dipped it flowered: petals of Lauder red swallowing flecks of white into a stiff stamen of hot yellow. A petunia. An egg, or a flower. In her mouth, it lived and softly died.

CHAPTER XVI

EGGS

He would walk into the newsroom with his arms full, piles of papers and books in one arm, a sack full of eggs in the other.

"You need eggs?" he'd ask. I always said yes, thus ensuring my spot on the list of first refusal. I'd pay my dollar and open the carton to check for cracks. The various colors—tornado blue, nipple brown, faded army green, Mary Kay pink—were so beautiful, so lovely together, and they still are. Like Easter eggs already dyed, but in Martha Stewart hues. He later raised the price to $2.50. A dollar was always a joke.

I would tell him how good his eggs were in frittatas, Spanish tortillas, in the linguine I made from scratch until I put too much flour into the mix and broke the extruder on my Williams-Sonoma pasta machine. I said we enjoyed them raw, drizzled over asparagus tips, and frothing up a batch of spaghetti carbonara.

"Yeah, well," John Wooley said, sizing me up, "they're pretty good fried, too."

John's wife, Janice, tells a great story about hens: When a coyote got in the henhouse and killed a bunch of Wooley's layers, he gathered the carnage up in a lawn-and-leaf bag to later bury, after a long day chasing country music stars by phone. But, when he got home, instead of burying the dead birds, he laid to rest a plastic bag full of old newspapers set out to be recycled.

He wrote country music for the local daily, and quit when he tired of chasing Carrie Underwood's eggshell ass all over Oklahoma. I miss how he'd walk into the newsroom all blustery, all business. He was and is the Eggman. (Sometimes Wikipedia is too funny not to quote: Eric Burdon, lead singer of The Animals, is claimed by some to be the Eggman of "I Am the Walrus" fame. The reason for this is that Burdon was known as "Eggs" to his friends, originating from his fondness for breaking eggs over naked girls. Burdon's biography mentions such an affair taking place in the presence of John Lennon, who shouted, "Go on, go get it, Eggman.")

"Can you drink today?" John would often ask. Wooley, I mean.

I loved to say yeah and then start ticking off the hours. When the happiest hour would come, he'd walk back by in the same willful fashion in which he entered. "If you're waitin' on me," he'd say, "you're backin' up."

I miss the way he'd berate me for whacking the penultimate paragraph from one of his stories, in order to fit the space, leaving the last graph to dangle like a paratrooper over enemy lines. I miss the swath he cut on the way to his desk, the bag of eggs swinging precariously between cramped aisles billowing with stacks of broadsheets and metal cabinets of bursting manilla folders. Of Leann Rimes and Nelson Riddles.

I enjoyed those Wooley eggs, I did. A John Wooley egg, like John Wooley, is a good egg.

An egg is basic, perfection in yellow and white. Look at the shape, feel the yolk, smell the white. You can't. An egg is odorless, even when treacherous. This, too, is a component of the perfect.

An egg is a canvas and paint all in one. *Eggja*, an Icelandic word, means "to incite." To egg on. Egg otherwise has Middle English origins, circa 1150–1475.

Jay Gatsby lived in East Egg. Nick Carraway, in West Egg, until he turned tail for home. Eggs are subtle mysteries until cracked.

When you pull an egg warm from the roost, which I did recently at a friend's farm, it's the very emblem of perfection, though occasionally one will emerge with shite or something smudged on it. Otherwise, the shell is smooth, clean and bone dry.

Eggs give in. I like the invisibility, the neutrality. What happens to an egg when it disappears inside a chocolate cake or a batch of Tollhouse cookies, where does it go and what is it doing? You can't taste it. You can feel it, perhaps, if you've the tongue for it.

An egg has a few basic, even familiar, parts. Let's crack one.

Shell

Bumpy and grainy in texture, an eggshell is covered with as many as 17,000 tiny pores. Eggshell is made almost entirely of calcium carbonate ($CaCO_3$) crystals. It is a semi-permeable membrane, which means that air and moisture can pass through its pores. Hold it up to the light and see for yourself. The shell also has a thin outermost coating called the bloom, or cuticle, that helps keep out bacteria and dust.

Inner and outer membranes

Lying between the eggshell and egg white, these two transparent protein membranes provide efficient defense against bacterial invasion. If you give these layers a tug, you'll find they're surprisingly strong. They're made partly of keratin, a protein that's also in human hair.

Air cell

An air space forms when the contents of the egg cool and contract after the egg is laid. The air cell usually rests between the outer and inner membranes at the egg's larger end, and it accounts for the crater you often see at the end of a hard-cooked egg. The air cell grows larger as an egg ages.

Albumen

The white, *albus* being Latin for "white." Four alternating layers of thick and thin albumen contain approximately 40 different proteins, the main components of the egg white in addition to water.

Chalazae

Opaque ropes of egg white, the chalazae hold the yolk in the center of the egg. Like little tethers, they attach the yolk's casing to the membrane lining the eggshell. The more prominent they are, the fresher the egg. It's Neo-Latin for "hail, lump."

Vitelline membrane

The clear casing that encloses the yolk. Why a yolk shines.

Yolk

The vitellus. The yolk contains less water and more protein than the white, some fat, and most of the vitamins and minerals of the egg. These include iron, vitamins A and D, phosphorus, calcium, thiamine, and riboflavin. The yolk contains lecithin, an effective emulsifier. Yolk color ranges from just a hint of yellow to a magnificent deep orange, according to the feed and breed of the hen. Vitellus means "calf."

Let us now praise famous hen

Breakfast orbits around eggs, with its sun-like yolk and enveloping universe of white. A recent *New York* magazine cover story titled "The Breakfast Manifesto" led with an egg— an over-easy in extreme, the orange-yellow orb of yolk glistening like a crown jewel. It looked as if, any minute, it would slide right off the page.

Inside, a trio of staffers laid out "the city's best morning meals" in 20 categories. Under "Eggs," featured were the just-set, Austrian-style of Blaue Gans on Duane Street: soft whites, bright-orange yolks "runny but not too." The eggs are served in a martini glass, "one nestled atop another like a pair of baby seals sunning themselves on a rock." Makes me wish I were a polar bear.

A place called El Beit, across the bridge in Williamsburg, takes the "Egg on a Roll" category. Flouting convention—an egg on a roll is little more than a scrambled egg, bacon, and cheap cheese sandwich—El Beit substitutes New York sharp cheddar for the American and scrambles the eggs to order with fried sage.

"Best Breakast, Period" goes to a place called Egg. "Soul-satisfying, all-American," Egg is another Williamsburg favorite. (Is this why so many of my friends have gone Brooklyn?) Range eggs, heirloom grits, buttermilk biscuits, and Col. Bill Newsom's artisan ham create a Gestalt irony—a country breakfast in Brooklyn.

An egg-cream, another New York invention, contains neither. It is a milk, seltzer, and chocolate syrup fizz.

The crack of dawn

Eggs were bound to be the first breakfast food, lifted as they were warm from the nest and cracked over Neolithic incisors on the spot.

No getting past it. When we eat an egg, we're eating nutrients—what the chick would get if it were a chick. Of course, it never really had a chance. Most of the eggs we eat, supermarket eggs, are never fertilized, commercial layers never getting, well, laid. All the same, it's strange. The yolk is the protein upon which the embryo would grow. Weeks later, out would hatch a yellow Nerf ball of a bird. Which came first, the chicken or the egg? The egg, at breakfast. And when you eat one, you're not eating an embryo—you're eating his lunch.

With a heart and mind capable of occupying its core, a fertilized egg is life come full-circle: It is where life and death converge to make food.

A tasty, two-egg scramble: Crisp some bacon in a skillet and reserve, leaving the fat in the pan. Take two eggs and blend them barely with a healthy teaspoon of milk or water. When the bacon fat is frothy, pour in the eggs. The bottom of them will set quickly—

use a spatula to lift the edges and let some liquid egg run beneath. Just before the top has cooked through, scoot the eggs back and forth to scramble and cook. Pour onto a warm plate while they still have some jiggle in them. Writes Aldo Buzzi: "The knack, for the cook, is to get the eggs to set but only just." Sprinkle chopped tarragon. Eat hot, with a glass of wine, if you have it. "This glass of wine will almost certainly be white," instructs Edward Behr in *The Art of Eating*.

Hard-boiled

An egg is a soul that makes soulful food. Watch Robert De Niro as Louis Cifer in *Angelheart* peel back and bite into an egg. Already he's got our attention; it's the way he peels the shell with those pointy nails of his. Eyes squarely on Mickey Rourke and into the camera, he bites, lunges really, latching onto the white as if it's still an embryo and showing traces of life. Then he chomps down and sucks the spirit out of all humanity, managing to keep all traces of shell, yolk, white and salt out of his black Van Dyke. Then Rourke takes the elevator back up to meet his fate.

I read somewhere of a dish called the Monster Egg but have since lost track of it. It required 15 eggs, separated, then brought back together again in the shape of a very huge, hard-boiled egg. It sounded like an immense amount of trouble for a football of an egg.

Scotch eggs are nothing more than battered-and-fried hardboiled eggs. After that you'd need a Scotch.

To properly egg

Finger the egg on its broad end, as the roundness lends stability. Keep the egg loose in the hand, not only to prevent crushing but also to keep from diverting the energy to the arm, where it is misspent. (Costner advised in *Bull Durham*, handing a baseball to the rookie Nuke whom he called "Meat," "It's an egg. Hold it like an egg.") An end-over-end trajectory is best—an egg held on its broadside will, when thrown, act like a curveball, an unacceptable occurrence given the intent. Aim somewhat high—the great majority of tossed eggs fall short of their intended target—and, without fear, follow-through. The egg is up to it and your throw will be all the better. Wait around long enough to see the results, but don't dilly-dally.

If you find yourself on the receiving end, see "How to Wash Egg Off a Car" at e-How.com.

The art of eating eggs

Edward Behr thought enough of the egg to put it on the cover of his book, *The Artful Eater*. He explores eggs for 14 some pages.

In baking: Behr notes their functionality—how they add volume to omelettes, brioche, Yorkshire pudding, crepes, popovers, soufflés, mousses, meringues, and puffs. "Whole eggs beaten into foam along with sugar raise a genoise, the classic cake that predates baking soda and powder."

On tells: The lower an egg floats in water, the fresher. A blood spot on a yolk he terms a "biological accident." A white will become wetter and less firm as it ages. A boiled egg will spin smoothly and a raw egg will wobble.

On stiff whites: Beat them in a copper bowl first cleaned with salt and lemon or vinegar "to eliminate grease and verdigris." A little sugar will bind with the water from the whites and keep the foam from separating. Even a tiny amount of yolk can stifle stiff peaks.

On hard-boiling: "Put them in cold water and bring them to a boil, boil one minute, then leave them, covered, off the heat for ten minutes." This will produce a soft but set center, what the French call *mollet*. (I tried this and got drier results than I'd hoped for. Nothing worse than a too hard-boiled egg.)

On risk: I quote Behr verbatim, to better capture his prowess.

"Without a raw egg, there can be no mayonnaise, since the supermarket product has almost nothing to do with the true olive oil-yolk-mustard-lemon sauce. And without a lightly cooked egg, there are no poached eggs to make wonderful combinations of yolk and sauce, no delicate omelettes, no custard sauces. The kind of risk we choose is cultural. By some American standards, Europeans accept unreasonable risk in consuming young raw-milk cheeses. The Japanese accept risk in the way they eat fish. Americans insist on nearly a fail-safe food supply, but on the highway we accept a huge risk in exchange for mobility."

Speaking of mayo, here's bistro Balthazar's recipe for mayonnaise:

2 large egg yolks
2 tablespoons Dijon mustard
2 teaspoons fresh-squeezed lemon juice
1 teaspoon sherry vinegar
½ teaspoon Worcestershire sauce
½ teaspoon Tabasco sauce
½ teaspoon salt
½ cup grapeseed oil
½ cup olive oil

Put all the ingredients except for the oils in the bowl of a food processor. Blend for 30 seconds. With the blade still spinning, drizzle the grapeseed oil in a very slow stream, followed by the olive oil. This should take about two minutes. As the mayonnaise forms, the noise from the food processor will become louder, making a slapping sound, as it does with cake batter. Process until the mayonnaise is thick, with a creamy body.

Mayo made thusly will refrigerate well for a week. Balthazar adds ketchup and substantially more mustard, Worcestershire and Tabasco to make Tartare Mayonnaise for the raw, chopped steak dish. Garlic cloves added to mayonnaise make aïoli, the staple sauce of Provence.

Keep 'em separated

Here's a great way to separate eggs that I learned watching *Who's Killing the Great Chefs of Europe?*

Crack it over a bowl and pour the contents into your hand, left dangling over said bowl. Spread your fingers slightly and shake your hand back and forth, letting the albumen fall into the bowl. You're left holding a perfect and free yolk. It probably won't look better in your hand than it did cradled in Jacqueline Bisset's, but it will separate.

Cool-Hand Luke ate 50 eggs on a dare and then passed out on the dining-room table—arms outstretched, palms and feet pinned to the rack by 50 chalky yolks and the dreams of the disenfranchised.

"I can eat ... 50 eggs," Luke promised the inmates as they cast their lots.

"Boy," said Dragline, "nobody eats 50 eggs." Dragline, the truest disciple, was so named because when he climbed into a ditch with a shovel, nobody could dig like that, not even a machine.

"I can eat ... 50 eggs," Luke swore once and for all. And so he did, with a little help from Drag, who massaged his gut between bites and tipped white after slippery white between his ever-greening lips. The doubting Drag, caressing the soft spot in the side of the master's swollen belly.

Of course, they crucified ol' Luke, but not before he revealed to them the naked, damned truth about life and how to live it.

My dad eats them runny—with the yellow bleeding yolk dusted heavily with salt and pepper—which might explain why I prefer mine super-fried, hard and crispy, the yolks sapped of all their nascent glow and the whites frizzled at the edges, what the Spanish call puntillas. The Spanish of Extremadura favor fried eggs with cured ham and crispy fatback. It's fitting that Spain does wonders with eggs, it being the home of such great ham. Eggs are like the Spanish, likely to take any shape, unlikely to conform, never bland, not even in an egg white. One painter— Pelayo Olaortua of Bilbao—painted several still-lifes of fried eggs as proof.

All Spanish, writes Iberian food authority Teresa Barrenechea, prefer their whites set and their yolks wet. Olaortua achieves this by cooking the white in a half-inch of olive oil until it starts to bubble. Then, with a spatula, he bastes the white with a bit of hot oil and very deftly spoons an indention in the white, into which he replaces the raw yolk. The entire egg is basted with hot oil for another 15 seconds, then lifted from the oil and plated.

American Southerners baste their eggs with bacon grease, but that separation of yolk and white prior to cooking is hundred percent Spain.

From Castilla come candied egg yolks: Yolks cooked in sugar syrup until they crystallize, after which the mixture is poured into a loaf pan and refrigerated overnight. The next day, the yolks are scooped and rolled—into ping-pong sized balls—in a coating of powdered sugar.

A distant, dead relative of mine ate brains and eggs. Shows you what stuff I'm made of. Rose brand pork brains come in a can with gravy. Rose is the brand North Carolina Congressman Howard Coble called for in his brains and eggs recipe for a congressional cookbook.

Eggs and brainless: the Egg McMuffin. A hand-held Benedict, plus a cheese single, minus the Hollandaise—the excuse for Benedict in the first place.

Killing time in the stylish concourses of Amsterdam's Schiphol Airport, I caught a televised report out of the corner of my eye: two masked men dumping and carting off dead, mad cow. It was the year of the terrorist, the season of the witch. The whole world seemed to have lost its taste for living. I touched down in Brussels a few hours later with a thirst for ale and a hunger to know: Was this the beginning of the end? I bought a London *Observer* in a kiosk strewn with soft-porn covergirls and read the first reports from Afghanistan while drinking a café noir. That evening, I drank a large Chimay, flexed a few mussels, then wandered endlessly around the Grand Place looking for my ride. In rather a panic, I fumbled with a phone card for an hour before finally finding him on the receiving end. I drank a Leffe Brun in a nearby café waiting for his car. We navigated the roundabouts and lanes back to Watermael-Boitsfort, dodging darkened cyclists. "Belgians are crazy about bicycles," he said. Later, on his sofa, I stared into the television at a Cradle of Filth video, the one where Dani Filth extracts his new bride's beating heart. I went to bed but didn't sleep until the plane out of Charleroi was halfway over France. I awoke with my face against the pane to see the castle of Carcassonne rise out of a sea of vineyards—a turreted ship scudding tempest waves.

CHAPTER XVII

WAKING BLAKE

Not long before he died in suburban Dallas, Blake bought me lunch at Tsunami Sushi at Second and Detroit. It was the summer of 2007, maybe June. I do recall the color of the sky (gray) and that the glass cube of Williams that reflected it—stuck in the downtown mix like a Lego castle in a mausoleum—was still the *future* home of City Hall. Blake died one day before Halloween, that's a fact.

I'd never eaten sushi for lunch. It seemed exotic for a work day. Tsunami is gone and in its place Yokozuna, where I recently lunched on a delicious pork-belly ramen, which would have been more Blake's turf in another time. After we ordered, he handed our waitress the calling card of the gluten-intolerant, for he'd recently been diagnosed with celiac. On it were printed the things that were not allowed to touch his plate. She read it quickly and pocketed it, with a confident nod that said this was nothing new to her.

We sat across from each other and avoided small talk, aiming instead at some higher level of hindsight that would not come. Not in a quiet sushi bar, at noon, over cups of green tea.

Blake brought up his book, a self-published, small-business consulting manual titled *Strategic Decisions for Small Business: It's Just Noodles, This Ain't No Trattoria*. When I laughed at and inquired of the title, he said I gave it to him. Meaning, he took note of something I said over a jug of wine and an impromptu pasta about 15 years prior. Then he asked about my own book—a vanity press job on a local entrepreneur—and all of a sudden the whole thing seemed remarkably sad and self-conscious, this fish lunch among delinquent friends.

These were not the books we dreamt of one day discussing, the ones we threatened to write during the heady, gimlet days when Blake made me sit and read Hemingway's "The Short Happy Life of Francis Macomber" as he watched, in order to gauge my first and truest impression. Distant was the night in an Arkansas fisherman's cabin with Blake cooking calf's liver and caramelized onions while I read verses of Whitman's "O Captain, My Captain," and another when we drank incessant sherries and discussed a piece of near-forgotten Faulkner.

Blake did not teach me to drink and eat, but he unveiled for me the precedents of culinary diviners past. From the get-go, he seemed to make it his responsibility that I know the method of steak au poivre, and that Gallo—"Not the house label, the Reserve," he instructed—made a good and cheap red table wine. He wasn't working with watery clay. Well before we met, I was into shaking my own martinis by formula and could tender a decent *boeuf Bourguignon* and a passable fettuccine al fredo (in fact, the first dish I ever cooked, the one I clung to like a pacifier for years). I was at least a formative lump of wet earth, the proper mix of minerals and soils worthy of a go.

Blake was employed by the same firm as my first wife, who shared his absorption of accounting principles if not his appetites for food and drink. "There's this guy at the firm you need to meet," she said one evening. "He drinks martinis." The first event was a dinner that he would cook in the borrowed kitchen of another co-worker, a tiny blonde and a husband who sold headsets but whose

15 minutes came in a tryout tending goal as a would-be Winnipeg Jet. We were six that night, half of us strangers if not for long. Much disaster and joy would ensue from this gathering, but it would be meted out deliberately and achingly over many months. All of it traceable to, if not because of, that first of Blake's many fitting meals.

He earned his master's in something financial at Tulane, but he majored in New Orleans. He'd dined at Arnaud's but preferred the less fussy Galatoire's on Bourbon. He was a three-tour veteran of Mardi Gras. Brennan's, I gathered, was his Valhalla, its eye-opening Sazerac his courage in a cup, its grillades and grits the wax that sealed his most precious tales of conquest. The sound of antebellum jazz—French in feeling, island in spirit, Gotham in its science—would stir his juices into a froth, a mirthful condition he would acknowledge with a great "Goddam, Brown!" if I happened to be within earshot. After which he would recline into a chair and close his eyes, as if resting between courses.

I'd never tasted a chicken Tchoupitoulas nor, to my knowledge, a Chateauneuf du Pape. Blake had been saving the bottles for years to impress the likes of us. I came to learn that this was not a typical practice for him. The Blake I got to know seldom cellared a bottle. "No time like the present" was his way of saying who knew when we'd have another, better chance to dive in than then and there.

We took seats, Blake near the kitchen, me at the one head of the table, the blonde at the other. While he plated the food, she poured the wine. The sauteed chicken breast sat atop a bed of diced and spiced potatoes, napped on one end with a velvety sauce Bearnaise. I stood in the kitchen before dinner to watch him bring it together. He kept a careful eye on it, resting on the back burner on a low flame, as if it might suddenly sprout mold.

I brought the glass to my nose and sniffed a delicate whiff of dust and decadence commingling in wedding crystal. I was all of 27 and to my tender lips—weaned on Foster's, scoured by Beefeater's—the wine seemed beyond me, like a dark, deep cave full of best-kept secrets.

Blake glanced over at me. My place at the head was a coincidental bit of foreshadowing that would play out later in scenes of frittered romance and broken homes, in cafes and bars and dance clubs all over town. To think it all began with a morsel of sauced chicken stuck on four tines. I bit and Blake studied my face for signs. I took a hit of the wine and winced at the forwardness of it, aggravated as it was by the meat in my mouth. I spoke, when I spoke, as a child.

Blake took a bite. As he chewed, his eyes rolled backward slightly into their sockets, the irises making half-moons. He ate with a satisfaction I had yet to embrace. But my time was coming.

Every vice needs a vehicle. Literature fueled our pursuits every bit as much as food and drink. Books were our hub and from it all manner of ideas took flight. In one particularly inspired fit, I wrote a long-winded analysis expressing my admiration for Henry Miller's *Tropic of Cancer.* I used big words, some of which I knew, to get to a place I wanted to go but had not the arsenal to get. In ten or so pages—which I bound with staples, as if I'd be turning it in for credit—I climbed the long, tall hill of Miller getting nowhere but lost and thirsty. Blake read it and praised it with his questions and pursed-lip perusals. Afterward, we shook an afternoon drink, aiming again at the symbol of Miller, albeit this time in terms we both could manage.

All our heroes drank to excess and we did our best to worship them. On fly-fishing trips, we'd sink our beer into the cold freshets as instructed by Norman Maclean, drink our whiskey like Bill Faulkner from pocket flasks pulled from flannel shirts, and shoot wine from botas, a la Hemingway, whom we took to calling "Big Ern." His *The Sun Also Rises* and its trout-infested Irati were never far from our thoughts, thoughts that rushed back to me in 2002 when, coming out of the plain of San Sebastian into the valley of Pamplona, I drove across the olive-green river and it left me wanting. Ern's Irati, I assumed, was higher up the hill.

Our wine we saved for evening fare, like any number of the addled authors of our recent reading. Our house red then was boxed Almaden, a faux "Burgundy" made passable by its 12-percent ABV and the sorry state of my palate. We drank better wine on occasion but the times dictated a lesser pedigree. About this time I began to think of wine not as something you opened at life's grand banquets but as an essential element to any meal worth eating. I ultimately moved beyond the Almaden, but I revere the sanctity of that first box the way saints revere communion.

One day when the gals were away, Blake called to say that it might be a great idea for me to come over, hang out, read, and then grill a steak in the night air that had grown cool and ripe from the advent of autumn. I never had anything in the way of plans in those days, which must be the windfall one accrues for not being mature, employed, and otherwise productive.

Buying a steak with Blake was like buying a car with your dad. He wants it to be your choice, your motivation, but he was there every step of the way, buying precariously to suit his own pursuits. We walked into Bruner's, now closed, and up to the counter and we couldn't have been there 10 seconds before the chosen one revealed itself: a Porterhouse of nearly two pounds. A $21 dollar steak, raw and red and ridiculously huge. And all mine, for Blake's long, thick New York strip was back in his refrigerator marinating in olive oil and garlic.

"That's a piece of meat, Mr. Brown," he said, approvingly.

The $21 was a heavy dent in those days, and if Blake hadn't been buying the wine and gin I likely would have bought a raggedy sirloin. Or lied and said I had plans.

Blake was a master at seasoning and preparing a steak. I bought that Porterhouse but quickly relinquished it into his loving hands. As he peeled it out of the butcher paper with another of those "Good God's!" of his, I poured myself a drink and him one too and retired to the library, which contained the set of leather-bound Hemingway hardbacks from the Easton Press that I'd sold to Blake a year prior in a moment of fiscal uncertainty. I sold a lot of things back then, not all of them to Blake: a Pentax SLR camera, a Schwinn 10-speed, a Toro mower, a queen bed. I tried like mad to sell my leather jacket to Blake's wife, who slipped it on and immediately seemed inseparable from it. Anyway, I still have that jacket.

As Blake seasoned steak, I cracked *A Moveable Feast*. In it were familiar friends with whom I could quickly escape in an afternoon's reading sandwiched around steak and Blake: Evan Shipman and his whisky saucers at the Closerie des Lilas, Ralph Cheever Dunning's cold-cream jar of pure opium, Ernest Walsh with the two French girls in long mink coats, Aleister Crowley in a cape, with a tall woman on his arm, strolling darkly up and down the Boulevard St.-Germain, the avenue of my dreams.

With the steaks marinating side by side in the fridge until the dinner hour, Blake joined me, probably with some Faulkner or Fitzgerald or O'Connor. If our authors seem obvious now, blame it on youth and catching up. In college, Blake studied formulae that dealt in probabilities and outcomes. I vaguely studied marketing, a thing less scientific and way more impractical, but I'd since fallen into the world of publishing in the most primitive manner possible. Together, we forged a common ground in the bathtub-gin Americans who wrote with a touch of the modern and bore habits that we liked to admire and sometimes childishly emulate. And this we did, untold peaceful minutes we stretched out over hours until they became a short set of years, a time when when most things came undone except Blake's desire to eat, cook and drink in my presence, which did not waiver.

Blake was largely a meat-and-taters guy who did not cotton to fruit with his meat. He didn't mind chutney as a curry condiment, but he didn't like it on his roast chicken the way some of the restaurants of the day did it. Any fruit belonged either at the end of the meal, with nuts and port and cheese if any were around, or in the glass. (Rich fruity red zinfandels were his favorite.) Nor was he terribly fond of dessert, for that was the time of digestifs, which for him sufficed as an end to things.

When I finally left his house that night, saturated and sane again, I did so fortified against what the rest of the week would deliver, melancholic that none of it would measure up to this, but happy that I was capable of recognizing that.

One warm-cool spring evening that just so happened to coincide with Mardi Gras, Blake and Cindy and I went out. (Cindy was the blonde, the one that hosted us that first night. By that time, she'd taken to hosting me in her townhouse.) It was not uncommon for us to go out, but typically Blake's wife Leslie would join us. That night, it was two against one, never a fair fight but, on Carnivale, a terrible mismatch.

The Mardi Gras before, we cooked chicken etouffee at Cindy's. At some point in the festivities, I attempted to open a window that time and paint had sealed shut. It popped open so violently that a pane ruptured and tore into my forearm. That sent us all to the minor emergency clinic, where the kindly nurse bandaged my wound and snickered at my aura of cayenne pepper and boxed wine.

We began our adventure at S&J Oyster Bar on Brookside, with a plan to eat oysters and drink bubbly, a plan rendered nonsense by the wall-to-wall reverie. We ran into two friends who'd arrived early enough to get seats and were now eating bowls of gumbo and jambalaya and drinking two-fisted. We exchanged holiday greetings and little else, swept aside in a strong current of young drinkers, and left them in there island of relative dining pleasure.

Working our way down the block, we drank a glass of wine at The Grapevine then found our way to Montrachet, our bistro of choice given that the magazine I helped produce traded ad space for food. There, we began a round of martinis.

Liz Taylor was behind the bar. She's the bartender who raised the stakes for me in the second wind of my newfound youth, and I have followed her in her various moves over town as best I can given the moment (easier as a bachelor, when she was at Camerelli's, harder as a parent, now that she's at Lucky's, in ironically the same location, though they shifted the bar from the end of the room to the middle). When she asked me if ever I'd tried a French martini, I switched my allegiance from gin to vodka for a season. I enjoyed as much the presentation: Liz would squeeze the orange peel over the cold cocktail and the acid would ignite and shoot sparks when she stuck a match to it. Lacking gin's medicinal flavor but packing much of its punch, a French martini is a dangerously drinkable thing.

We did manage to eat something, though food that Fat Tuesday was not the dominant theme. I'd usually order the fettuccine with mushroom-madeira sauce because it was the cheapest dish on the menu but also because the leftover sauce kept the waiter coming back with crusty, complimentary baguette. I carbo-loaded my way through relative poverty that way for months on end. Or I ate soup and bread, which made me feel like Jean Valjean from *Les Miserables*, which made me feel considerable.

Whatever we ate that night was not enough, for it was late and there was too much firewater under the bridge. We'd gone from liquor to wine and back again with obvious results. Blake and I rode a tide of crashing froth into shore and collapsed into a drowning pool of pebbles, weed, and salt. The mood at the table went from celebratory to vindictive like a screen door slamming in a rogue wind.

Cindy, the sober voice of reason, lost patience and grew fangs. I called her the "C" word and Blake snorted in both horror and approval. She bolted the table in a huff to drive home without us. After a few minutes of calm assurance, we paid our tab and left. Out on Brookside, we took off on foot north until at least the park, cutting across along the snaky Terwilleger Boulevard by the ponds where happy brides pose for common portraits. Only it was pitch black. We scraped along, hangovers on the horizon, closing the gap between the present and the inevitable confrontation that awaited me a mile away.

A new chemistry was emerging, gradually, like a sauce emulsifying. A restlessness had crept in and all around came a recognition of the end times. Fazed and confused, I found myself torn, between Cindy, after my affections, and Blake, after my appetite. Thus squeezed I withdrew, and by late summer our sun had set.

Leaving a lover is an uninteresting episode lent interest by the unsavoriness of emotion. The ties that untidily bind boys and girls slipped free one at a time that final summer, leaving minor slashes that finally cauterized and healed themselves as naturally as is allowed. Cindy and I emerged as friends of a sort, then blended into history. Leaving Blake was less clean, as clean goes in such messes.

Unlike with romances of the heart, a friendship built on food is not readily requited by some new object. There are not plenty of fish in that sea. With no obvious replacement for our shared appetites, we carried on, if with fewer meals and further between. Usually we'd meet for a drink, or once it was to drive golf balls. On that range, I was Blake's superior—he'd only taken up the notion in order to go on dates, what with Leslie now out of the picture (her exit was gradual and rather predictable, but torturous all the same)—and the fit was not good at all. It did not suit us, me being the expert in things. My lessons in how to swing a golf club without hooking or slicing were no match for his in how to deglaze a pan, lift a soufflé, or bind a sauce. Our common terrain was the kitchen, pure and simple, and he was boss.

We met again one happy hour for the sole purpose, it was revealed, of plotting some strategy for his entrée into the slippery world of the singles ads. And on that note I clumsily withdrew from his life. A new set of friends was taking up more of my time and I let them, until Blake and I made do with an occasional phone call, a tentative date to meet and do something, and then nothing.

I'd moved on, taken his lessons, his laughs, his lush brotherhood, and shelved them as I did the Library of America volumes of Lincoln, Sherman, and Adams I collected and planned to retrieve when, one day, an opportunity for more relaxed reflection arose.

We met again, a couple of years later as Cindy was about to make her Dallas exodus—a decade and then some before Blake made likewise—and I cooked a recipe I'd clipped from the newspaper, an old 15th Street Grill linguine dish featuring green-lipped mussels napped in cream and nestled into a bed of wilted spinach. In the galley kitchen of my new digs, I was trying to chop mushrooms, talk, and drink champagne at the same time and doing none of them well. Cindy nudged me aside, stole the knife from my hand and started chopping, a scene that Blake found humorous enough to acknowledge, while retreating from the kitchen all the same. It would be like him to harbor just a pinch of shame for me in a moment of acquiesence such as that. I did not see it that way, but then our ideas about women never were as compatible as those about food.

Blake had a wonderful new girlfriend in tow who was crazy about the North Carolina Tarheels—an odd fit indeed—but Leslie was there, too, it being something of a sendoff. We ate and drank with nothing really to discuss, at least nothing anybody would admit to. Things did not get out of hand, not in the least, and it felt not joyous but at least not treacherous. The Tarheel fan had for me a copy of Joyce's *Dubliners* that she'd bought at Shakespeare and Company on a recent trip to Paris. It was one of the Dover paperback editions and I was reading the contents page when she tried to explain her efforts to buy it in hardcover, only they didn't have any on display and when she inquired the bookseller—an angry old man not Sylvia Beach—nearly bit her head off.

"Big deal," I said. "It's from Paris." The rest of us only acted as if we'd been there.

Before I forget, Blake was a big ol' boy, not horribly obese but not very firm or athletic either. His neck puffed like an adder's, his cheeks were full, and his eyes almost misty with appreciation, I liked to think. He tucked in his shirts and was very tidy about his parted hair. He did not play sports (unless horseshoes is a sport) or enjoy watching them televised. His idea of a big day was not the Final Four but, rather, going to shop for an attachment blade on his Cuisinart.

"You should see them, Brown," he said of the potato slices he'd made for a buttery pommes Anna. "Perfect eighth of a fuckin' inch!"

I don't know what became of the Tarheel, but I know Blake had remarried by the time we'd caught up over sushi. He was about to follow his wife to Dallas, where another job always seems to await. I don't think all the boxes were unpacked before I got the e-mail.

What had changed about him most, as he sat across from me drinking his tea and nibbling at the plate of something hopefully not gluten-contaminated, was the face. The body too, as he was thinner all around. But the face has a way of displaying this first and foremost and to me Blake's face looked smallish, triangular, and drawn, and his eyes like the embers of a campfire of the night before, when you wake up and stir them remembering the warmth and glow of only hours ago.

As he talked of his book and idly of his new wife and stepchild, I had to work to come up with responses to topics that seemed remote and untethered. I struggled to make stories of my one-year-old sound endearing but ultimately stopped, and added that line of conversation to the gathering heap. The dialogue dipped and dragged until the hour or so was up. When Blake paid the check, it felt like a public-relations lunch that rambles indelicately and ends with an equally vague sense of what to do next. Out on the corner, annoyed by traffic, we fought for a way to call it a day.

"Thanks for lunch, man. Me next time."

"You're welcome," Blake said warmly. "Don't be a stranger."

I was almost across the street when he yelled over, "And let me know when that Hasty-Bake book comes out, Mr. Big Round Balls," invoking our favorite Bobby Peru line from David Lynch's *Wild at Heart*, a scene we must have recanted a hundred times, with Nicolas Cage balking at climbing into the El Dorado, Isabella Rossellini done up alien-slutty in frosted hair and comically heavy eye-liner, and Willem Dafoe, snaggle-toothed and pencil-mustached, about to blow shotgun holes in local yokels.

That night, after dinner and some discussion of the day's odd proceedings, I poured a glass of malt whisky, in spite of the warmth of the evening. I'd been working my way through the variety of Islays and Speysides and Orkneys, attempting to locate in the nose and finish the difference between distilleries often separated by mere yards. Scotland was a small place, as my map of the Whisky Trail indicated, and yet so much variety over so pure a creation and so traditional a method.

I sipped and sniffed at the peat, salt and sweet—a sweetness that by all accounts should not be there, given the prescription of ingredients—and contemplated Blake after all these years. It had been 11 of them since I had seen him, which did not seem possible.

It's possible, likely even, that I drank another glass the night a few months later after the day I got an e-mail from Blake's wife telling me he'd died in the night and that she thought I'd probably want to know. He was 42. It was only an e-mail, a brief couple of sentences from a woman I'd never met. Still.

Blake and I, when we drank brown liquor, tended to drink bourbon or Tennessee whiskey. We drank Dewar's but not with passion. He once got onto me for favoring Jim Beam over Jack Daniels, really for just wanting to know why I'd go to the trouble. I didn't have the guts to tell him that I'd seen a Beam ad in a British lad mag called *The Face* and that was why.

We did not drink Scotch single malt then because we didn't know much about it and couldn't have afforded much of it even if we did. Which is fine. In my experience, malt is something to drink *after* you've arrived, wherever it is you're going. It was Dewar's, a blended Scotch, that I carried in my pocket flask on our fishing trips. We took turns pulling from it as we sat in the chest-high rushes of the Mountain Fork River where it empties out of Broken Bow Lake to make its way 'round Beavers Bend, bending naturally, lazily toward the high cliffs.

I sat in silence with my fly rod out of the water where it was even less threatening to a trout, because what angler could argue with that on a gorgeous, golden October afternoon with Robert "Blake" Hendrix swatting the river up ahead, the sun just eclipsing the cliffs, and a dinner of something pan-fried and wine-friendly to come?

A goat cheese, a chevre, gains ferocity as it moves through time. At three days, it's barely more interesting than a Philly cream cheese. Its light, fluffy texture makes a nice, neutral bed for flowery honey and wild berries. At three weeks, a rind begins to develop around an interior that has grown more pungent and robust and begun to reflect the earth upon which the beast has been fed. At three months, most of the moisture is gone and the disc is now flat as an Oreo. The only way to eat the rind, at this point, is to grate it onto a salad or some eggs. Its flavor is tongue-numbing, saline and fierce. What little cream is left within the pate is ripe, if not rank, and tangy as all get out. It crumbles on the tongue, dry as cotton, and yanks mightily on the salivary glands. As the cheese warms in your mouth, it takes on the full flavor of the raw milk from whence it comes. At this point, you are on your own to discern the taste of that.

Mark Brown is managing editor at This Land Press. He publishes *Argentfork*, a food-and-drink quarterly, from his home in Tulsa, Oklahoma.

SELECTED READING

Chester Aaron, *Garlic is Life* (Ten Speed, 1996).

Colman Andrews, *Catalan Cuisine* (Harvard Common, 1988).

Teresa Barrenechea, *Cuisines of Spain* (Ten Speed Press, 2005).

Edward Behr, *The Artful Eater* (Art of Eating, 2004).

Anthony Bourdain, *A Cook's Tour* (Bloomsbury, 2001).

Aldo Buzzi, *The Cuisines of Spain* (Bloomsbury, 2006).

Julia Child, Louisette Bertholle and Simone Beck, *Mastering the Art of French Cooking* (Alfred A. Knopf, 2001, 50th Anniversary Edition).

Child with Alex Prud'homme, *From My Life in France* (Alfred A. Knopf, 2006).

Eleanor Clark, *The Oysters of Locmariaquer* (Ecco, 1998; first published in 1959).

Sophie D. Coe and Michael D. Coe, *The True History of Chocolate* (Thames & Hudson, 2007).

Barnaby Conrad III, *The Martini: An Illustrated History of an American Classic* (Chronicle Books, 1995).

Jeff Cox, "California Olive Oil," *The Art of Eating*, 2006.

Frank Hamilton Cushing, *Zuni Breadstuff* (Heye Foundation, 1974).

Elizabeth David, *A Book of Mediterranean Food* (New York Review Books, 2002; originally published in 1950).

Marlena De Blasi, *A Taste of Southern Italy* (Ballantine, 2006).

Patrick Dillon, *Gin, The Much-Lamented Death of Madam Geneva* (Justin, Charles & Co., 2003).

Chloë Doutre-Roussel, *The Chocolate Connoisseur* (Jeremy P. Tarcher, 2006).

Patrick Faas, *Around the Roman Table, Food and Feasting in Ancient Rome* (Palgrave Macmillan, 1994).

M.F.K. Fisher, *Consider the Oyster* (MacMillan, 1941).

Barbara Jeanne Flores, *The Great Book of Pears* (Ten Speed, 2000).

Betty Fussell, *The Story of Corn* (Alfred A. Knopf, 1992).

William Grimes, *Straight Up or On the Rocks: The Story of the American Cocktail* (North Point Press, 2001).

Melissa Guerra, *Dishes from the Wild Horse Desert* (Wiley, 2006).

Peter J. Hatch, *Fruits and Fruit Trees of Monticello* (University of Virginia, 2007). U.P. Hedrick, Cyclopedia of Hardy Fruits (Macmillan, 1922).

Fergus Henderson, *The Whole Beast* (Ecco, 2004).

Peter Kaminsky, *Pig Perfect* (Hyperion, 2005).

Mark Kurlansky, *The Big Oyster: History on the Half Shell* (Ballantine, 2006).

Shirley Line, *Oysters: A True Delicacy* (MacMillan, 1995).

Keith McNally, Riad Nasr and Lee Hanson, *The Balthazar Cookbook* (Clarkson Potter, 2003).

Prosper Montagné, *Larousse Gastronomique* (Crown, 1961).

Susan Pinkard, *A Revolution in Taste: The Rise of French Cuisine* (Cambridge University, 2009).

Claudia Roden, *The New Book of Middle Eastern Food* (Alfred A. Knopf, 2000).

Waverly Root, *The Food of France* (Vintage, 1992; first published by Alfred A. Knopf in 1958).

Root, *The Food of Italy* (Vintage, 1992; first published by Alfred A. Knopf in 1971).

Mort Rosenblum, *Olives: The Life and Lore of a Noble Fruit* (North Point, 1996).

Rosenblum, *A Goose in Toulouse* (North Point Press, 2002).

Rosenblum, *Chocolate: A Bittersweet Saga of Dark and Light* (North Point Press, 2004).

Rebecca Rupp, *Blue Corn and Square Tomatoes* (Garden Way, 1987).

John Tebbel and Anne Seranne (eds.), *The Epicure's Companion* (David McKay, 1962).

Dennis Tedlock, trans., *Popol Vuh: The Definitive Edition of the Mayan Book of the Dawn of Life and The Glories of Gods and Kings* (Simon and Schuster, 1985).

Henry David Thoreau, Walden (1854; Library of America, 1985).

William Woys Weaver, *Heirloom Vegetable Gardening* (Henry Holt, 1997).

Weaver, *Sauer's Herbal Cures* (Routledge, 2001).

Edith Wharton, *Italian Villas and Their Gardens* (De Capo, 1976; originally published 1904).

Paula Wolfert, *The Cooking of Southwest France* (Wiley, 2005).

ACKNOWLEDGMENTS

A hearty salute to all the *Argentfork* subscribers over the years. Like King Harry's small band of brothers, you are a most devoted tribe. Hail to the chefs, Philippe Garmy and John Phillips, and cheers to Tom and Liz. Much appreciation to all at *This Land*, to Jeremy and Carlos and Courtney, and to Cecilia and Claire for tidying up. For always coming to the table: Bret and Cynthia, Louis, Robert M., Anibal, Jeff K., many delicious others. To Jim Fitz for trying, and Jeff Martin at BookSmart Tulsa. Thank you Michael and Suzanne. Thanks, Vince. To my colleague and champion, Michael Mason, who believed without seeing. For Ken and Bonna: A mother and father go a long way toward setting the table. And again to Kelly Kurt, my missus, for eating and reading whatever I throw at her. Finally, lovingly, to Lucas and Jonas—for earning their ice cream.